Finding David

AN AMERICAN WIFE BETRAYED
BY HER GOVERNMENT

Carol Hrdlicka

POW Hrdlicka
Conway Springs, Kansas

David Hrdlicka

Carol Hrdlicka/ POW Hrdlicka
www.powhrdlicka.com

Book Layout ©2017 BookDesignTemplates.com

.

Finding David: An American Wife Betrayed by Her Government/ Carol Hrdlicka. —1st ed.
ISBN 978-0-578-93929-2

Acknowledgements

My gratitude goes out to Bill Lunn, Emmy Award-winning anchor and reporter in Minneapolis, Minnesota, for his exhaustive interviewing and recording of the documents and notes that have constituted this long work in progress. "Many of the details in this book are subject to Carol Hrdlicka's best recollection. Tremendous research, interviews, and the review of dozens of documents went into this book." - Bill Lunn

I also appreciate the manuscript formatting guidance of Di Finch, Ph.D., United Nations ghostwriter and editor.

I would like to acknowledge some of the people who were all instrumental in helping me over the years: Former Congressman John LeBoutillier, Ross Perot, Sydney Schanberg, POW family members, POW activists, Jerry Streeter, and Roger Hall. Hugh Turley and David Martin were instrumental in getting the book over the finish line.

There are a number of unnamed others who contributed, including people who gave interviews. I also very much appreciate the solid support of our children, David, Denise, and Damian.

Be sure to visit David's webpage powhrdlicka.com for more information and documents. Go to the "Timeline," where there will be highlighted words in blue, click on those words and documents will come up. For more documents go to the "important document" heading. A special thanks to Yelka Mikolji of Indigo Technologies for her tireless effort both on the webpage and with this book.

To my beloved husband, David Hrdlicka, POW,
and to all the other brave POWs & MIAs, abandoned by the U.S. government in Vietnam and Laos.
We will never forget you, America's betrayed heroes

"I can come to no other conclusion...
In 1973, some were left behind."

— Former U.S. Secretary of Defense
James Schlesinger, during
Congressional POW/MIA 1992 Hearings
Admitting that POWs were knowingly left behind in Vietnam and Laos.

Praise for
Finding David

This heart-touching and inspiring true story is a tribute to American fighter pilots and all soldiers abandoned at the end of our undeclared wars fought on the Korean Peninsula and throughout Indochina. Filled with indisputable facts, it cries out to faithful Americans to never, ever permit betrayals such as this criminal act to stain our honor again.

The telling of this demand for loyalty to men and women serving in harm's way, specifically if taken prisoner, could be titled: "David and Carol vs Two Goliaths." "David" is Captain David L. Hrdlicka, a USAF fighter pilot shot down over the Ho Chi Minh Trail on May 18, 1965, during the CIA-run secret mini-war in Laos. "Carol" is David's loyal young wife, mother of three preschoolers at the time.

Goliath #1 is the "Evil Enemy" USSR, China, North Korea, North Vietnam, Laos, etc., are all still evil, even after the glorious 1989-1991 partial meltdown and freeing of East European, Baltic, and Balkan and South Siberian nations. But over 1 ½ billion people are still not free.

Goliath #2 is tragically our own bureaucracy, military and political, uniformed and civilian cya-careerists, embarrassed by failure, lying, lying and then lying about lies. But the worst of the deniers of truth are a pair of US Senators and a few U.S. House members who shamefully don't have time to investigate or "it's a long time ago," all unworthy of holding office.

"Leave no man behind," the honorable battle cry of every noble army when victory is in doubt is now, itself, in doubt in this country.

Does brave Carol Hrdlicka uncover the truth? Does she unravel the confounding and scandalous cover-up of hiding the "alive" status of her David during so many years of his detention by a hostile power? See for yourself. Every faithful American should read this chronicle of a truly spiritual battle!

- **Robert K. Dornan**, former Congressman and former U.S. Air Force wingman of Capt. David L. Hrdlicka

Carol's War Room

Carol Hrdlicka is one cool, courageous, and feisty lady. She has taken on members of Congress, the military, and the State Department in her quest for information about her prisoner-of-war husband. For 56 years she has sought answers from a country that would not release him and from a country that could not or would not retrieve him, and she will continue to do so.... until her last breath.

W. Jerry Streeter, David's schoolmate

Contents

Prologue

Over Sam Neua, Laos May 18, 1965

The red lights came on, lights no pilot ever wanted to see, especially in combat. Captain David Hrdlicka saw the glow at the top of his instrument panel. He gritted his teeth. An alarm sounded simultaneously. What they meant was that his aircraft was on fire. He could not see or feel any flames. The fighter pilot instinctively maneuvered his F-105D Thunderchief skyward. If he had to bail out, he wanted as much altitude to do it as possible. He had just dropped his payload of bombs onto a road, a supply route for the Viet Cong in Laos. Hrdlicka has been hit by ground fire before. A few weeks previously, a .50 caliber round had ripped through his fuselage just four feet behind his seat, severing part of a hydraulic line, striking, but not penetrating his belly fuel tank. He'd saved that round as a keepsake. The "Thud," as the F-105D was known, was a tough aircraft. It could take a licking and keep flying, but now, fearing he'd been hit again by ground fire, he asked his wingman or any of the other three pilots who were flying with him that day from the 563rd Tactical Fighter Squadron flying for confirmation.

"I've got a fire warning light," Hrdlicka announced.

"Roger, flight leader, you're on fire."

David Hrdlicka had made a promise. I had warned him for years about those pilots who tried to be heroes by steering their troubled aircraft away from villages or population centers, only to die themselves by waiting too long to eject. Part of his combat training called for piloting even a severely damaged aircraft as far from the target area as possible. After all, one thing was certain at a target area. The enemy was below. In Laos, even getting over a ridge or mountain pass might be the difference between an enemy village or a friendly one. Despite that, Hrdlicka remembered his promise to his wife. He reached for the ejector lever and he and his seat were jettisoned straight up from the aircraft. The force was violent, and the fighter pilot now felt himself hurdling out of control more than five thousand feet above the ground. He was still attached to the seat, but suddenly it separated from him while his chute deployed simultaneously. In seconds, his parachute stabilized his fall and slowed him to a drift. Hrdlicka now floated above the Laotian landscape. He looked down and scouted for a place to touch down. It was mostly green, dense, and lush. Around him were mountains. But below him was an open area near a village. What waited below for this young husband and father of three small children was anybody's guess.

POST-CAPTURE PHOTOGRAPHY OF
CAPTAIN DAVID L. HRDLICKA, USAF

Part I

CHAPTER 1

I Chose an Air Force Pilot to Love

It was 1965 in Wichita, Kansas. David and I had been married for nine years. David had the rank of captain as an Air Force pilot. We had only two days' notice of David leaving for Vietnam. That meant a lot of scurrying around to get affairs in order. We had just taken over the handling of a ranch in Montana. David was going to be gone for four months, so I asked him what I was to do with the property, and he told me to just follow what he had written down in a ledger. I was 27 years old and had three small children at home.

At the time, we were also in the process of moving into a new house, which was supposed to be finished in a couple of weeks. David and I had spent months watching the building of that house. The morning he left, it was bright, warm, and sunny, but our mood, as you might imagine, was not. With only two days' notice of departure, though, we had little time to think about what it all meant. Maybe that was deliberate on the part of the order-givers. But, then, it was just to be a brief separation....

He'll be back in four months, I assured myself. After kissing David goodbye, I watched him walk across the lawn to the waiting military car. At that moment, a strong feeling came over me that I would never see David again. My heart ached as I waved one last goodbye. *I'm being silly,* I told myself. *I'm just worried about all the impending responsibility I now face.* The sedan drove away, and I turned and forced myself to face the challenge that David would expect of me until he returned.

I met David Hrdlicka on a blind date in 1953 in Littleton, Colorado. Morris Evans, a high school upperclassman and friend, asked me if I would go out with David. I told him I would as long as it was a double date. David was 22 at the time and I was 16. *That's an old man,* I thought to myself. I knew some of David's six siblings and had even gone on a date with David's younger brother, Ted, who was just a couple of years older than me.

The night of our first date, David picked me up at my house. Mother didn't allow me to meet anyone anywhere. My expectations for the date were low. I'm not sure why; maybe I was just intimidated by the age difference. When David came inside the house, he immediately introduced himself to Mother. In front of me stood a very handsome, well-dressed, well-mannered, solidly built United States Air Force airman. And here I was, a high school student. What's to compare? I could easily tell that mother was impressed, to say the least, with David's demeanor. He was so well-mannered and following rules, whether they be Air Force regulations or Mother's regulations regarding me, made little difference. The first date consisted of a movie followed by a trip to the local hamburger stand. After the date, David politely walked me to the door of my home.

"Enjoyed the evening, Carol. Goodnight," and he turned and promptly walked back to the car without waiting for a response.

I awakened the next morning and realized that the date had been a success. I liked David's attitude! Thinking back now, he was a true officer and a gentleman. *"Eat your heart out, Richard Gere! David's more handsome than you."* Still, I tried not to get too excited. *He'll either ask me out again or he won't,* I told myself. He did, and from that point forward we spent nearly all of our free time together. As our dates continued, we would drive all the way to Denver to a fish and chips place to feast on battered cod. For me, having grown up on a ranch in Eastern Montana, life with David was full of new adventures. He took me to my first formal restaurant. There were even white tablecloths. We had lobster! I admit I took a long look at the red crustacean when it arrived at the table. If you've ever known anyone who grew up on a ranch or farm, you will understand my dilemma. *Oh my God, what am I going to do with this.*

CHAPTER 2

An All-American Son

David Hrdlicka was born on December 30, 1931, in Stewartville, Minnesota. He attended St. John's Prep in Collegeville, Minnesota, where he graduated in 1950. He enlisted in the Air Force on February 10, 1951. He completed basic training at Lackland AFB, San Antonio, Texas, aerial gunnery training at Lowry AFB, Colorado, and B-29 Superfortress combat crew training at Randolph AFB, Texas. He was a tail gunner aboard a B-36 bomber. He and his crew would sometimes go on 36-hour flights taking pictures and performing other reconnaissance duties. I believe they flew over Russia as part of those missions. David had first served as a B-29 Superfortress crewmember. He then climbed aboard the newer B-36 with the 24th Bomb Squadron of the 6th Bomb Wing at Walker from March 1952 to August 1954, and then serving with the 40th Bomb Squadron of the 6th Bomb Group.

When David wasn't logging long hours aboard bombers, he'd drive home to Littleton on leave for two weeks. When he'd arrive home, I would see him every day. When we were at my house, Mother was happy to have him. She thought he was wonderful. She had no man to help her around the house and David would come over and jump right in and complete handy projects that included repairs. Mother greatly appreciated it.

David also brought me to his house in Littleton to meet his family. We spent a lot of time at David's house, sometimes hanging out there all day. The Hrdlicka house in Littleton was a flurry of activity. The house was modest with three bedrooms and one bathroom. There were eight members of the Hrdlicka family. Father Theodore was a prison guard at the nearby federal penitentiary in Littleton. Mother Maxine ran a sewing and clothes-making business out of the home. The Hrdlickas had seven children, six boys and a girl. David was the oldest, followed by Teddy, Tommy, Gretchen, Johnny, Leo, and Chris.

I was soon a frequent guest at the home. At the height of the Cold War, I walked up to the house one day and found David's father, Theodore, hand-digging a nuclear fallout shelter in the family's yard. He was using a spade and had enlisted the help of a few of David's brothers and some other boys from the neighborhood. I wanted no part of the dirt and shovels and found my way inside to see David's mother.

Maxine made money for the family by making dresses and doing repairs and alterations for people all over the Denver area. She had a sewing room in the house, and in that room was a big oak table that she used for cutting the material. I took a seat on the table and chatted with Maxine while she was sewing. She showed me a number of shortcuts and tricks I would later find valuable. Maxine was an attractive woman with hazel eyes who never left the house unless she was well-dressed. She made all of her own clothes, and clothes for her daughter as well. Her beautiful dark hair was beginning to turn grey.

With Maxine using a room for her business, there wasn't a lot of extra room in the Hrdlicka home. The six Hrdlicka boys shared one bedroom with bunk beds, though David was not normally home. Meanwhile, sister Gretchen got her own room. Some of the boys razzed her that the arrangement wasn't fair. She teased them back by pointing out they took more time in the bathroom than she did. There was a daily battle for the one bathroom. Eventually, Theodore's fallout shelter would be converted to a finished basement with a second bathroom.

Theodore Hrdlicka was handsome, well-groomed, and very strict with his boys. Working as a prison guard, he wanted to make sure that none of his boys wound up under his control at work. He was less strict with his daughter. She thought her Dad looked like movie star Robert Taylor. Mr. Hrdlicka was never the picture of health. He smoked a lot and had terrible migraine headaches. He eventually became a recluse in the house, spending most of his time in the basement. Once down there, he didn't come up and didn't communicate much. In a like manner, the kids did not communicate much about their feelings to their Dad. He was distant, and the kids didn't infringe on his thoughts and feelings. He loved his family but was so strict that in some ways it drove them away. The Hrdlickas were Roman Catholics. Mrs. Hrdlicka had converted to Catholicism for marriage, but on Sunday mornings it was she who made sure her six boys and daughter go to church.

The family had moved to Littleton from Sandstone, Minnesota, around 1949. David stayed behind in Minnesota to finish high school at St. Johns, staying as a boarder. He graduated in 1950 and immediately enlisted in the Air Force. Because of this, he was not home very much, but whenever he would come home it was very special for the Hrdlicka family.

With David spending nearly all of his time with me, sister Gretchen was growing jealous of my presence in David's life. Gretchen was David's number one girl until I came along. But we still got along very well, as I did my best to stay sensitive to her feelings for David. Eventually, we became close friends. I understood Gretchen idolized her eldest brother, and in a like manner, David was very attentive to her.

David was courteous and thoughtful of everyone, and I never knew him ever to be critical of a soul. He had a lot of friends and got along well with them all. When he came home from the Air Force, it was something to celebrate. During this time David taught Gretchen how to drive using his car. It was new, a two-tone Ford hardtop, dark green on the bottom and light green on top. David was particular about his car. Once when he was about to give Gretchen a lesson, she slammed the car door very hard.

"You're gonna pull that door through the other side!" he hollered at her.

Gretchen steered the car around the neighborhoods of Littleton under David's watchful eye, and he gently coached her on the finer points of being a good driver. During these times when David was home on leave, Gretchen tried so hard to please him. One day she picked up his military shoes that he normally spit-shined. She wanted to impress her brother and do something nice for him, so she took a brush to the shoes. *They look nice, but I'll shine them up even more,* she thought. When she was done and showed him, she thought he was going to die he turned so white in the face. He reacted with a stern look, speechless.

"It was nice of you to do, but don't ever do that again."

Gretchen felt bad, but David wasn't one to hold a grudge. He polished his shoes all the time. He got out the black shoe polish and a cotton ball. He'd spit on the shoes and go to work, and he'd have a mirror shine by the time he was done.

And to prove he didn't hold a grudge against his beloved sister, David put on a record in the family's living room and he taught Gretchen how to slow dance, their feet sometimes getting tangled up causing them to chuckle. She was 14; he was 23.

But David could also call out his little sister. One time while home on leave, he noticed that Gretchen had gained a little weight.

"You better watch out. It gets harder to lose the older you get."

Leave time was precious to David's family and me. He would often entertain us all playing his saxophone, sitting on a stool with his toes curled under the lower bar.

Then as quickly as he had arrived, he'd be gone again. We would exchange letters and talk on the phone as much as possible during the interim.

CHAPTER 3

Strong Willed and Independent Early On

The dynamics of my nuclear family couldn't be in more contrast to David's. We lived in Montana. My brother, Joe, was two years older than me, and we had an alcoholic father. He and my mother fought constantly, and the marriage finally ended in divorce. Mother, a schoolteacher, then became pregnant out of wedlock and the conservative Miles City, Montana, school district had a decision to make. As a teacher, she had signed a morality clause. Having a baby out of wedlock would be in violation of that agreement. Mother decided the best thing to do was to leave town. She loaded up the car, and we drove to my Uncle John's ranch in Dulce, New Mexico, where mother left my brother and me with Uncle John and Aunt Grace. She then drove to Albuquerque where she stayed for two months, giving birth to my sister. Mother returned to pick up my brother and me and we started driving north. We stopped in Littleton, Colorado. Mother decided Littleton would be home for her and her little family. Home in Littleton was 157 Logan Street, two blocks from the high school. I have no idea why she picked Littleton. I suspect she didn't, either. She might have simply run out of money or, perhaps, the car ran out of gas. It could have been as simple as that.

I stayed full of resentment for a time about having to leave Montana. I was a ranch-raised kid and I loved my horses. I had free run of the town in Montana. I'd ride bikes, disappear all day, shoot bows and arrows. That was my life that came abruptly to an end. In like spirit, I refused to go to my new school in Colorado. Mother had to literally drag me out of the car and into the 8th grade classroom.

Dad turned the ranch in Montana over to his brother after the divorce. The fight over the ranch ended up in court. As it turns out, in the State of Montana at that time, you could not willfully disinherit minor children. The court ruled that the ranch was to be turned over to my brother and me when I reached the age of 21. Mother was hoping that through her kids, she would eventually get control of the ranch. Grovanna Bradshaw—my mother's name—was obsessed with the ranch, and she was going to own it, one way or another.

The years passed, and by the time I was 16, I had met David and through the years we had fallen in love. Though Mother learned to love David, at first things didn't go so smoothly. Mother could see that David and I were becoming more serious, and she started to have second thoughts about where this romance was going. She was worried that I was much too young for David.

But I was bound and determined, not only to date David, but to marry him. This teenage belligerence was new to me, but not to my mother. I was as headstrong as she had proven herself to be. It came back to haunt her. I was generally a rule-follower and had never previously challenged mother on anything—well maybe once or twice—but my sense of self was firmly asserting itself in the growing pains of rebelliousness.

Meanwhile, David's enlisted career in the Air Force was coming to a head. He made staff sergeant while serving at Walker Air Force Base. But his commitment was nearing its end and he had a decision to make. He mulled over getting out of the Air Force altogether. But then an opportunity arose to take the test for the cadet pilot training, a pathway into the glory job of the Air Force without a college education. David was a very bright young man and passed the test with flying colors. Had he not, he would have certainly ended his Air Force career and moved into civilian life, but passing the pilot's test gave him a new focus, renewed energy, and a motivating goal.

David received an honorable discharge from the Air Force on February 9th, 1955. He then waited six months before heading to pilot training. Most of the other trainees were either college graduates or had some years in college, and David knew that he would have to work harder to prove himself, to show that he was pilot material.

David and I continued to date when he would take leaves to come home. While he was gone, we again wrote letters and talked on the phone. I was now attending college at the University of Denver.

Quarrels with Mother did not stop but progressed from bad to worse when I started talking about marriage. Mother expressed concern about my age. Yes, I was only 17, and it had only been a year since David and I had met, but I was mature for a 17-year-old. Yes, David had not proposed. It was more of a plan for a couple of years down the road. In fact, on one of David's trips to Europe, he bought a set of wedding rings. Yes, he had bought them before we ever started dating, but it just shows how fated we were for each other.

There were more intense confrontational fights with Mother. I knew what she wanted when it came to David. She feared losing her control of the ranch if we were married. But

I was willing to fight for David. I threatened to run away from home, but it was during one particular confrontational fight with her that I yelled,

"I'll get pregnant...and then I'll have to get married!"

"If it weren't for the ranch, David wouldn't be interested in you!" she blurted out.

Like I said, Mother would do anything to take control of the ranch. But Grovanna Bradshaw would never forbid me from seeing David. She knew I was just as tough as she was, because I'm her daughter. That would have been the end of our relationship. Mothers don't think there is anything that would come between themselves and their daughters, but the love of a man certainly can and will. In me, she had raised a tough and determined teenager who would not allow her to come between me and my love for David. Little did I know at the time that that kind of determination and willpower would serve me well during the biggest battle of my life on a world stage.

CHAPTER 4

Why Me, David?

July 1955

David took a break from the Air Force for a few months but then entered the Aviation Cadet Program on July 14th, 1955.

David and I became engaged during Christmas 1955. There was no formal proposal, no dropping down on one knee. He handed me my ring wrapped as a Christmas present. David and I were two practical-minded people who had simply put together a plan to be together for a lifetime. Looking ahead, our plans depended on David's Air Force career.

David chose me, I believe, because I was fresh clay that he could shape exactly as he wanted. I never knew what David's experience was with other women, but with me, David led the relationship, and I wanted him to. I had not had a father to look up to, and David was the first man I could respect, and I did respect him. I looked up to him to have the answers from day one. When I looked at David, I saw a level-headed and trustworthy guy. The fact that David was brilliant was an added asset.

During this time, David also worked at a plant in Littleton. He made a prototype he would work on, gluing toothpicks together to build it. The prototype he was building would do his job mechanically.

"David, that's not smart, you're making a machine to do your job," I warned him, but of course, he clearly knew that. He was only staying there for six months and then moving forward with the Air Force. When he finished the prototype, he gave it to the company and didn't charge them a cent.

"You know, before giving it to them, you could have patented the design and then sold it to them instead," but I knew David was aware of that as well.

He didn't care. That's the kind of guy he was. He was completely focused on becoming a pilot, and everything else was irrelevant. He was just biding his time to go to pilot school and if adding interest made his present job more enjoyable, so be it.

David was also taking pilot lessons at the Bar None Airport in Littleton before he went for pilot training. Every time he would come home, there were two things he wanted to see: Me, and my competitor, a Piper Cub airplane at the nearby airport in Littleton. He would go there every time he'd come home on leave with the intention of working toward his private pilot's license. I spent a lot of time sitting out at the airport while David flew with an instructor. After he got his license, he would take me up and fly into a powder puff. We played a game where we would look for holes in the clouds and when we would spot one, David would maneuver the plane, either climbing or diving through the hole. We would do acrobatics. While I was scared the first time I went up, I did not want David to know. I especially didn't want him to know that his tricks, loops, twists, and dives bothered me. I trusted David implicitly and knew that he would never hurt me or put me in a situation where I could be hurt. In the Piper Cub, it was too noisy for us to talk, so we carried on our dates aloft in oral silence. Knowing that flying made David happy also made me happy. But sometimes I felt that I had a rival in the airplane. Once back on the ground, I made an observation:

"David, if airplanes were humans, I wouldn't stand a chance."

David made no comment. He would later leave to go back into Air Force pilot training, and he didn't come home as much.

Littleton, Colorado, November 1956

David graduated from cadet pilot training at the end of October 1955 and was commissioned a 2nd Lt., awarded his pilot wings at Laughlin AFB, Texas, on October 30, 1956.

We drove back to Colorado. Our wedding was already set up. We were married in Littleton at the Catholic Church, November 3rd, 1956.

"Do you, David Louis Hrdlicka, take this woman to be your wife?"

David, a devout Catholic, was nervous and slow to answer.

I couldn't believe what I wasn't hearing. I elbowed David hard in the ribs, urging him to answer the question.

"I do!" he replied.

* * *

I was 19 when I married David on November 3, 1956, at St. Mary's Catholic Church in Littleton, Colorado. My uncle, John Pettus from New Mexico, took the place of my now deceased father in giving me away. David's sister, Gretchen, served as maid of honor. David's brother, Ted, was best man. David's mom, Maxine, made my beautiful wedding dress.

After the wedding, guests went to the Hrdlicka's house, but again, the Air Force was calling. Just hours after saying our vows, David and I climbed into his two-tone green Ford and rambled southwest from Littleton to Luke Air Force Base in Phoenix, Arizona. As we drove through the mountains, it started to snow. It came down more and more heavily. The driving became hazardous, and we finally had to pull over when we got to Raton Pass in southern Colorado near the New Mexico border. We spent our wonderful honeymoon night at a motel in the middle of a mountain snowstorm.

David and Carol Hrdlicka wedding photo

CHAPTER 5

Fighter Pilots Bond

George Air Force Base, Victorville, California 1957

Lieutenant Hrdlicka was assigned to the 1st Fighter Day Squadron at George AFB from June 1957 to March 1958. His next assignment—also at George, which closed in 1993—was with the 34th Tactical Fighter Squadron from March 1958 to March 1959. Then came an assignment as an F-100 pilot with the 308th Tactical Fighter Squadron, which lasted until September 1960.

Lifting off the runway in a pair of F-100 Super Sabres and flying out of the Mojave Desert in darkness, David and his wingman Bob Dornan steered their aircraft skyward and headed southwest. When they cleared the surrounding mountains, David saw a glow on the horizon, the lights from the city of Los Angeles. David had arrived at George AFB about six months after Dornan and was assigned as Dornan's wingman. They had become fast friends.

On this night, Dornan was giving Hrdlicka his first night checkout. With Dornan leading, the tandem flew southward, and they were quickly over the twinkling lights and massive spread of the city of Los Angeles. After passing over the city lights they flew out over the ocean. Dornan showed off some acrobatics doing a series of rolls, but always keeping his nose pointed in the direction of the ocean. He would later explain to Hrdlicka why he did this. The pilots then circled north, flying their Super Sabres over the Palos Verde Peninsula.

The Air Force pilots then flew up the coastline of California, past the pier at Santa Monica with the Ferris wheel. They passed over Beverly Hills where Dornan had grown up, a dark triangle, the lights covered up by the dense canopy of trees. They flew north along the Santa Monica Mountains, following Sepulveda Boulevard, eventually passing over the San Fernando Valley. Flying over the mountains, the pilots then headed northeast back toward George AFB. Once clearing the mountains, they could see two more groupings of lights. They then descended and practiced several night landings. They landed their aircraft and walked over for a debriefing.

Hrdlicka prompted Dornan about some of his acrobatics at night. Dornan had some advice. He explained that keeping his nose pointed out toward the ocean, if his engine stalled, he could at least bail out over water and his jet would not be a danger to the dense population below in the Los Angeles area. But an ocean bailout would come with its own set of complications.

"And then what?" Hrdlicka asked.

"You get your boots off and swim to shore. Or you hope some surfer comes out and helps you, Dornan smiled.

"Oh wow! I know I'm in a fighter squadron now," teased Hrdlicka.

They both chuckled. Dornan was growing to like Hrdlicka. They were just getting to know each other, but they were becoming best friends. Dornan had a new idea. Hrdlicka did not yet have a call sign in the squadron.

"You know what your call sign should be?"

"What's that?" asked Hrdlicka.

"Hard liquor," said Dornan, smiling, noting the similarity phonetically to Hrdlicka.

"Naaaah, I don't drink that much."

Dornan realized his friend was right, as clever as it would be, he couldn't stick him with that call sign.

Their helmets were white, with reflector tape red lightning bolts on the side.

Lady Fury...picture of David...hanging off the side of an F-100...the helmet on the canopy...Dornan's helmet was near David's shoulder...Dornan took the picture. They took each other's picture.

Dornan's wife and I went up in the tower to watch David and Dornan do air-to-air and air-to-ground maneuvers.

The squadron all had bird names. They would all pick raptors – Eagle, Hawk, Falcon.

Radio...talking to Dornan:

"Falcon lead, can you give us a legal flyby"

"Stack high."

They would fly at high speed just a few hundred feet off the desert floor.

The members of the control center that controlled all the flights in L.A. area were all out on the railing of the tower as they buzzed by.

"Go AB...Now!" Dornan ordered.

They both hit afterburners...felt the boom...flames shot from the back of their aircraft and they pulled up and headed skyward.

They were in.

Easter Sunday 1958, George AFB California

Hrdlicka and Dornan were attending Catholic Mass at the base chapel at George AFB, Easter of 1958. The priest asked Hrdlicka and Dornan to do the readings which they eagerly agreed to. After the Mass, Dornan leaned over to Hrdlicka and commented on his style of piously pressing his hands together while awaiting communion.

"David, I notice you're doing what I'm doing. You hold your hands together with your fingertips touching like an altar boy. I love that." Dornan commented.

"You know, everybody on this base, the doctors, nurses, the law office, the housing office, the simulator, every mechanic, everyone who puts the rockets and the bullets into our airplanes, they are all here to put us in the air," Hrdlicka replied.

"You mean, we're the star quarterbacks?" Dornan countered.

"Absolutely," said Hrdlicka. "We're it. So when we go up to communion and we come back like altar boys, all these families of the enlisted people and all the support officers, they're all looking at us and thinking, 'If they can do that and do the readings, I guess there's nothing wrong with me doing it.'"

That hit Dornan. While the image of a fighter pilot might be of swaggering out to the flight line like a cowboy, carrying a helmet instead of a lasso, sometimes involving rumors of womanizing, Dornan realized that the best thing they could do on Sunday was to show piety and humility. A small symbol of that was to return from communion reverently with their fingertips together and pointing toward heaven.

* * *

Another flight had Hrdlicka and Dornan flying cross-country. When some of the F-100's started logging long hours, they were due for maintenance. The facility that overhauled the fighter jets was at Seymour Johnson AFB in North Carolina. The Air Force policy was called IRAN, Inspections and Repairs, as Necessary. Dornan and Hrdlicka were assigned to fly two of the F-100s to the facility in North Carolina. The plan was to drop the aircraft for maintenance and return to George on a larger transport aircraft. They planned the trip in two legs, first flying to Biggs Air Force Base in El Paso, Texas, and from there to North Carolina. They did not have air refuelers yet. Flying across the Western United States, they admired the beauty of the country they had signed up to defend. They tried to maintain what they called "RD" or radio discipline as they flew. But Dornan had a thought, and he couldn't help sharing it with Hrdlicka.

"David, did you like Buck Rogers?"

"Absolutely!" he replied.

"You know what?" We've strapped rockets to our backs, and we are flying 10,000 feet over the airliners."

Airliners in the late 1950s would top out around 30,000 feet. David and Bob were at just over 40,000 feet in their F-100's – nearly 8 miles high as they looked down at about a third of the United States.

"And we're up here with the angels. I dreamed about this when I was a little kid, strapping a rocket to my back and flying up here," Dornan continued, "and we get paid to do this."

Hrdlicka was touched by the observation. He felt the same way.

"Stop making me feel guilty," he replied.

* * *

On another training flight, Hrdlicka and Dornan were flying over the Grover Cleveland National Forest not far from San Diego, California. This was Navy territory, and sure enough, within a few minutes, they could hear some Navy pilots chattering on the radio. Dornan had an idea to have a little fun.

"Eagle Two, go to channel 333. Listen to this Navy chatter," Dornan urged Hrdlicka to listen in. Once on that channel, Hrdlicka clicked his radio three times to let Dornan know he was there without talking and giving themselves away. As the naval pilots talked on the radio, they gave away their position.

One of them mentioned a landmark. Hearing that was all Dornan and Hrdlicka needed. Dornan, as the flight leader, wiggled his wings, indicating to Hrdlicka to follow him. And down they went, looking for those naval aircraft. Minutes later the Air Force pilots spotted two Navy Cougars below them, big and blue and easy to make out against the brown and green earthly backdrop near Ontario, California. They pulled in behind the two Navy jets. Dornan engaged his radio on the same channel now that the Navy pilots had been chattering on.

"Navy Cougars, you're both dead," Dornan announced. "Air Force Super Sabres at six o'clock. Check your six."

"Roger, we're dead," replied one of the Navy pilots, a conciliatory tone in his voice.

* * *

Hrdlicka and Dornan went on a training mission with their squadron commander off the California coast over the ocean. They took off in the dark just after sunset. The new commander, James Robinson "Robbie" Risner, was a war hero and ace who had shot down eight MIGs in Korea.

They took off in their Super Sabres and Risner said to them, "Drop back Falcon Flight, I want to show you something," Risner said. "AB...Now!"

Risner hit the afterburner on his aircraft and from behind David could see a purple tongue of flames about 30 feet long come from the rear of the F-100. Around the flames were white concentric rings getting smaller and smaller toward the rear of the tail of flames. In the darkness the flame and concentric rings were beautifully visible. They normally didn't see the effects of the afterburner during the day. Hrdlicka and Dornan then both hit their afterburners to keep up with Risner.

The training operation called for intercepting a B-52 that was posing as a Russian bomber somewhere off Santa Barbara. Dover 44 was the B-52's call sign. The B-52 was likely out of Castle AFB in California. After several minutes they homed in on the big bomber. When they had it in visual contact, they each rolled in and did a simulated gunnery pass.

"You guys shot me down," came a radio transmission from the B-52.

* * *

Bob Dornan would later say of David as a pilot, "He was as good as it gets. Solid as a rock. Cool at all times. Fun to work with because he enjoyed it so much." David had a career that Dornan himself longed for – went to England and flew the F-101 Voodoo. In David, Dornan saw a man "who was easy-going and always friendly, good-natured, but focused on the job. David was serious in pre-flight briefings. He was very focused during flight, and yet fun in the debriefing. David enjoyed all aspects of the flight. He was 'A fighter pilot's fighter pilot – a guy you'd always want to have on your wing.'"

Dornan once landed his F-100 on Bicycle Lake at Fort Irwin after losing his hydraulic system. For saving the plane he was subsequently named pilot of the month. David was impressed.

"Dornan, you're supposed to bail out if you lose your hydraulics," Hrdlicka said, "You get close to the ground in some wind gusts, you'd be on your back dead."

"David, I did that once and the canopy slammed me in the face harder than you can imagine."

The incident had kept Dornan from flying for four months, something he didn't want to have to do again.

While David had something of a fly-under-the-radar personality, Dornan was flamboyant, more of what you might expect from a fighter pilot, and that was displayed when he traded in his '53 Oldsmobile for a '55 black Cadillac Eldorado convertible. David took one look at Dornan pulling up on the base in the flashy ride and shook his head at his friend.

"I don't know if I could take the criticism from our commanding officer to be driving to work in a nicer car than he has. I couldn't take the heat," David said.

* * *

While flying the fast and agile F-100 was exciting, there was a new program being offered to Air Force pilots that sounded even more exotic. On July 29, 1958, President Dwight D. Eisenhower signed the National Aeronautics and Space Act, establishing NASA. Word went out to qualified pilots to apply. One day in the George Air Force Base flight room a group of pilots had gathered and were discussing it. Joe Engle, David, and Dornan talked about the possibility of becoming astronauts. Dornan and Engle said they were willing to give it a shot. Hrdlicka said he was quite happy being a fighter pilot. Engle was chosen, it having been deemed that he had the "right stuff." Dornan was not. Engle ended up a space shuttle pilot. Ted Freeman, in their squadron, was also chosen. Freeman was killed in 1963 while flying a T-38A trainer that collided with a flock of geese in the fog near Houston, Texas. He was the first fatality among the Astronaut Corps.

* * *

On the F-100, Dornan says, neither he nor David ever "rat-raced" around. Part of the culture was that with the macho persona of being a fighter pilot there were always a few who cheated on their wives. David and Bob did not like it. Dornan says it was a small, but unfortunate, part of Air Force culture among guys who were flirting with death all the time.

David Hrdlicka and F-100

CHAPTER 6

Moving Up Fast

The squadron was being put to the test to see which pilots would have the best gunnery scores. The scores were both air to air...a B-26 would tow a target over the desert and the F-100s would dive at the target taking shots. They would also practice and be tested on ground targets. When the testing was over the top pilot in the squadron was Wayne Fullam of Tennessee. Hrdlicka and Dornan were highly competitive and wanted to know what Fullam was doing to get the best gunnery scores. They confronted him.

"What are you doing, Wayne, to pick up your gunnery scores like that?" Dornan asked.

"I'm going to the gym and doing a lot of bicep and forearm curls. And when I'm holding that stick, my hand is a vise," Fullam replied.

David and Bob took what Fullam said to heart. They started going to the gym and did forearm curls and regular curls, and military presses and built up their arms. After a period of weight training, their gunnery scores also went up. They practiced air-to-air gunnery over the Mojave Desert 5,000 feet up, and 5,000 feet out from the target. They would roll toward the target and then reverse roll and bring the nose up...he describes more about flipping up the trigger, and you would feel the G forces on the stick, but working out gave them more power in their arms and forearms for working the four 20-mm cannons in the F-100.

Ten years later, Wayne Eugene Fullam would be shot down in his F-105D Thunderchief 32 miles from Hanoi. Fullam parachuted into the trees and was not heard from for decades. He was declared missing-in-action over North Vietnam. His family believed for many years that he might have been taken prisoner of war. He remained missing-in-action until 1988, when his remains were returned to his family.

But back at George AFB there was a goodbye party. Dornan sat at a table with David and me. Robbie Risner was also there. He asked Dornan to say a few goodbye words. He stood up and said,

"You know...they say the odds of being a fighter pilot are the toughest in the military. Only three out of every four hundred who want to be an Air Force pilot...only three are accepted, and only two of those three get to a pilot's rating. And 10% of those two get to be fighter pilots. And of those fighter pilots...only a third of those get to be better than their last landing."

Sometimes the tails of their F-100s would drag or rub the runway causing sparks to fly 100 feet behind the plane during night landings.

"You're only as good as your last landing," Dornan warned Hrdlicka.

"We have to kiss the runway every landing," David replied.

After that they would compare notes on the quality of their touch downs.

"Hey David, how was the landing?"

"Kissed it in," David replied, "Just a little squeak from the tires."

Their time wound down together at George Air Force Base. Dornan left to become an actor in Hollywood, a job, he joked, where the odds were even harder than becoming a fighter pilot. He would return to the California Air National Guard and that assignment would put him in contact with his best friend again, but in a way that he never would have wished.

Meanwhile, Hrdlicka received a new assignment that Dornan was envious of, new training in the Air Force's latest aircraft, the F-101 Voodoo, and an assignment ready to carry nuclear weapons into the Soviet Union. David and I and our young son, David Jr., born September 1957, were headed to London.

CHAPTER 7

F-101 Voodoo Mission

Bentwaters AFB England 1959

David's next assignment was a big one. At the height of the Cold War, Captain Hrdlicka was assigned to a new aircraft—one that is little known—whose purpose would have been to deliver a nuclear bomb deep into the heart of the Soviet Union.

The aircraft was the F-101 Voodoo. The Voodoo was 67 feet long with a 39-foot wingspan. Unlike the F-100 David had been flying, the Voodoo was equipped with twin engines. It also originally boasted four 20-millimeter cannons, but that was reduced to three by the time we got to England. It was developed as a nuclear-armed fighter bomber for the Tactical Air Command (TAC). An F-101A set a number of world speed records for jet powered aircraft, including fastest airspeed, attaining just over 12 hundred miles per hour.

* * *

While in England, David and I welcomed a daughter, Denise, who was born January 23, 1961. Then we had another son, Damian, who arrived August 2, 1962. Young David, Jr., was growing up. David, Jr., has told me how he enjoyed going on glider rides with his Dad in England. His Dad would joke that his son was the perfect ballast. It was the kind of glider you'd pull with a rope attached to a car to get airborne.

Another fond memory of David, Jr., at the time was of his dad helping him set up rabbit cages. We lived in Grundesburg, just a short drive from the base.

David's Mechanic 1959-1963

The crew chief at Bentwaters was Airman 2nd Class Kenneth McLaughlin. The crew chief was responsible for pre-flighting—checking all systems to be sure they were functional, making certain that tires were serviced, making sure there was oxygen in the system, conducting all maintenance, refueling and servicing—and post-flighting the aircraft. As a general aircraft mechanic, himself, David had learned the basics of the aircraft on the flight line. Up to then, there was no special training for the F-101. They all had to learn on the job.

About the 101, "She had quirks. She was a lady and you had to treat her like a lady," said Crew Chief McLaughlin, from Pennsylvania. "If you didn't fly it by the book you were in trouble," he said, "she was easy enough to fly, but you had to do it by the book."

Changing the tires was the biggest pain. You had to take the doors off to get to the tires. The F-101 could fly on one engine, but there were tough lessons to be learned. One bit of advice: Don't fly fast and flat on a gunnery mission. Instead, attack at an angle. The squadron commander found this out the hard way. During an air-to-ground gunner training mission over Scotland, the commander, attacking at an angle, flew into his own shots when he pulled out, picking up his ricochets coming off the ground and sucking up a 20-mm slug down the intake. He called in that he had a rough engine, shut it down, and flew back toward Bentwaters. When he got within about 50 miles, he tried firing the engine again, but it was running so rough and causing so much vibration that he had to shut it down again. When he landed and Chief McLaughlin and his crew checked it out, they found that of the plane's three engine mounts, two had been completely sheared off. It took them three days to rig a system to get the engine out. As a final note, they even discovered mud on the F-101's windshield or "windscreen" as they call it over there. The squadron commander had been flying so low and at such a great speed that the ricochets had also sprayed dirt back up into his windshield.

* * *

In the mornings at Bentwaters, there was usually a lot of ground fog and it was cold and wet, a lot of moisture in the air. By about 10 a.m. it would burn off and generally remain clear. Summer was nice. The days were long; it didn't start getting dark until around 9:30 p. m.

Some British civilians worked on the base. All facilities were on base, officer's club, NCO club, base cafeteria, PX, and commissary. Chief McLaughlin, like us, lived off base. The only time McLaughlin saw Captain Hrdlicka was when he came out to fly. Crews and pilots didn't associate. That was considered taboo at the time in the Air Force. The only time they associated with one another was when they were on alert duty.

Not only were there nuclear weapons on the base at Bentwaters, but there were also nuclear weapons permanently attached to aircraft. When the Cuban Missile Crisis occurred, Kenneth McLaughlin was on alert duty. They had converted trailers that had been made into bunk rooms and they were next to the Ops Office. One of the guys got up at night to go to the latrine facility. He stepped outside the door and encountered an AF policeman with an Alsatian guard dog.

"You better go back inside. This place is locked down."

They had listened to Kennedy's speech over the radio the night before. From Bentwaters, an F-101 could be in Russia in 20 minutes with a nuclear weapon. They knew if Russian missiles were launched at them, they had about 20 minutes of survivability. The nuclear weapons were loaded on aircraft. They had 12 aircraft from two squadrons on alert duty that were loaded at all times. They never flew with the nuclear weapons attached, though. Those never left the shelters. They had a special area; nuclear weapons were kept in a munition storage area. There were some 70+ such nuclear weapons at Bentwaters at the time of the Cuban Missile Crisis. A few, David had been told, had been sent back to the U.S. for modifications.

The aircraft were kept in open bay hangars, even the 12 loaded with nuclear weapons. They were kept separate from the other aircraft.

With Bentwaters being a very high-alert station, the crews were on a status known as Victor Alert 24/7, that is to say, all the time. If they heard a claxon go off, they grabbed the big screwdriver they used to close up panels, jumped on a crew truck and were delivered to their individual hangars with the air crew. They could not get into the hangars without the pilot. They went into the hangars in pairs. No one could go in by himself. A pilot McLaughlin was working with once forgot to put the forms that went with the aircraft. A crewman noted casually,

“Oh, he forgot the forms.”

“Mac, where are you going?” asked McLaughlin.

“The pilot forgot the forms.”

“Well, you're going to have to come back because you’re not going back into the hangar without those forms.”

McLaughlin ran a very tight ship.

* * *

When David crossed paths with McLaughlin they would chide each other. David knew that McLaughlin loved the F-101. It was the first airplane he’d ever had that had his name on the fuselage as crew chief, and McLaughlin took great pride in that. David would bug him…

“This Model-T,” David joked, because he had grown to love flying the F-100; he was sorry to get transferred.

“This is the Cadillac,” McLaughlin would reply, referring to the F-101, not a “lead sled,” referring to the much slower-flying F-100.

But Hrdlicka preferred the F-100 when he first got to Bentwaters. The F-100 had lugs that locked down the canopy. They used the loops/lugs to hang their strap on the hooks –

not what it was intended for. The hooks were in the F-100; it just worked out that way. Hrdlicka would say that it was better in the F-100 cockpit.

"What are you complaining about? We hand you the straps," says McLaughlin.

"Yeah, but in the 100 I could do it myself,"

"But you're getting topflight service when you're flying a Cadillac instead of a Model-T," McLaughlin razzed.

If they were on alert duty, they might have spent more time together, but, as it happened, David never had alert duty with McLaughlin. Still, it was important for the pilots to get to know the air crew. There's a day room, a lounge for ground crew and pilots, to play cards and watch T.V., so cordial relationships were encouraged as time went by.

"There's Joe Doakes...oh, shoot, I get him again..."

But most of the pilots were really neat guys. Some could be jerks and even condescending to the ground crew. Some thought they were God's gift to the Air Force. It was generally the younger pilots who acted that way, until they got a lecture from some of the older pilots. McLaughlin was present when a major got after a young lieutenant.

"Look Lieutenant, you're badmouthing the wrong people. They're the ones that maintain this beast, and all they gotta do is screw it up one time and you're dead."

McLaughlin said David was respected by the ground crew because he treated the ground crew as his equal and realized the importance of their jobs.

Along with his service as an F-101 Voodoo pilot with the 91st Tactical Fighter Squadron at Bentwaters from September 1960 to January 1963, David served as flying training officer for the 81st Support Group at Bentwaters from January 1962 to October 1963. His orders then sent us back to the United States as an F-100 and F-105 Thunderchief Pilot with the 563 Tactical Fighter Squadron of the 23rd Tactical Fighter Wing at

McConnell AFB, Wichita, Kansas. David had ended his dalliance with the lethal Air Force "Cadillac" for good.

CHAPTER 8

Dad David

McConnell Air Force Base, Wichita, Kansas 1965

By the spring of 1965, we had three children and were excited about building a new house just a few minutes from McConnell AFB. We lived in a rented rambler about five minutes from the base.

David was tickled to death about having young sons. But he was not particularly fond of babies, appearing to relate more to two or three-year-old children who could walk and talk. David was a man of his time – a chauvinist. I can say that, since I'm his wife. He wanted no part of changing diapers. I think David was raised on the advice, "If your wife asks you to do something you don't like to do, make such a mess of it, she won't ask you again." If I left David babysitting and his son would mess his diapers, he wouldn't change them. He would wait, hoping I would come home soon. If he absolutely had to change them, he would make such a mess of it all over the bedspread, that I got the message, loud and clear – when it came to changing diapers, I'm on my own!

David ran to keep himself in shape. He'd run wherever he could, even on the tarmac at the base. He wasn't fast and he didn't run exceptionally long distances. He was 5'10" tall and naturally muscular and strong. He did not lift weights but looked like he had been doing so for years. He played handball and had a collection of trophies from tournaments in the Air Force. David had blue eyes and always wore his hair very short in what he called a flat top. And, while he stayed fit, after we were married, I learned his favorite recipes from his mother, and his weight ballooned to just under 200 pounds.

David often used the kitchen table at home as the place to stress education with the kids. This was at the original house on Wicker Lane in Wichita before we moved to a new home. Even at age seven, David Jr. was interested in aviation. He would later grow up to be a fighter pilot like his dad. David Jr. often asked his dad about flight, and how aircraft floated through the air. I remember one particular day he asked his dad about the Air Force Thunderchiefs.

"What makes those airplanes stay in the sky when they roll like that?"

The fighter pilot and father responded with an elaborate diagram of a fighter jet with stick figures, representing air flow, on both sides of the wings to explain pressure differentials. He explained that the guys on the bottom of the wings have to run faster than the guys on top of the wings. And while David Jr. eventually understood what Dad was talking about, the immediate lesson learned wasn't an aeronautical one. His conclusion: "Be careful of the questions you ask Dad, and make sure you have a bit of time to hear the answer."

Yes, Dad David had the appropriate answers to all David Jr.'s questions and predicaments in which he found himself.

One day, Dad placed David Jr. on the roof and the young son then walked to the edge and looked over. Now it looked miles down.

"Come on. I'll catch you."

"You won't," David Jr. replied.

"Yes, I will."

"No!"

Eventually, David Jr. worked up the nerve to jump and his Dad caught him.

Still another time, when Dad would arrive home, all the neighborhood kids would be out playing in the street or someone's yard. Young David ran to see his Dad, who picked his son off his feet and pulled him against the outside of the car, then, holding his son tightly up on the outside of the car, he continued driving home about 15 mph down the street.

Once, the kids had a helium balloon that they were playing with in the front yard of our house. But David, just home and still wearing his flight suit with his characteristic change jingling in his pocket, grabbed the balloon from them and was now working on undoing the knot. He intended to inhale the helium and show the kids how funny his voice sounded. The balloon was brown and unusually large. But as David struggled with the knot, the balloon slipped out of his hands. He was standing on a three-foot tall block wall along the driveway. He made a valiant and athletic effort jumping after the balloon, but it was just out of reach of the fingertips of his outstretched arm and it drifted away. David Jr. and all the neighborhood kids stood in silence and watched as the balloon drifted skyward. He wasn't angry at his dad for losing the balloon, nor was he embarrassed in front of the other neighborhood kids. Instead, he felt sorry for his dad that he was trying to show the gang something neat, and it didn't work out. They continued to watch the balloon for a long time as it became smaller and smaller. David said his dad would have explained why the balloon was rising, explaining the physics and science involved.

"Can you still see it?" He would ask the kids.

"No, we can't see it," They all responded in unison.

"I can still see it," Dad said.

CHAPTER 9

Abrupt Departure

David came home the afternoon of April 5th, 1965 and announced that he'd be leaving for Vietnam in two days. That created chaos at our home for the next 48 hours leading up to David's departure. We were involved in a flurry of rushing around to get things done. David wanted to give me power-of-attorney over our affairs, but he had been advised that he wouldn't be gone long enough for me to need it. However, David still insisted that I be given a one-year power-of- attorney. He also borrowed some money to help me better manage things at home. I was lucky on both counts that David had forethought.

I busied myself doing David's laundry and getting his clothes ready to go. We were still living in the rental house on Wicker Lane and had planned to move into our new house just one block over at 1013 Blackwill in just three weeks when it would be finished.

The day before David left, I was worried about a variety of things. That's what I was good at – worrying. But I had one message for my husband as he was packing to leave.

"Don't try to save the airplane at the cost of your life."

"Oh, I won't. I won't. I promise."

I also pressed David about avoiding torture. The idea of David in enemy hands and being brutally tortured was more than I knew I could take.

"I'll tell them what they want because as soon as I hit the ground, whatever I know is obsolete," he assured me.

I gave David that advice on bailing out of his aircraft many times over the years, but I knew David's attitude would be to try to save the airplane. I always felt that if there was a problem with the aircraft, David would stay with it, despite my urgings to bail out right away.

The morning David left for Vietnam, a dark-colored sedan, an official Air Force vehicle, pulled up to the front left of the lawn. There were already some other pilots in the car for the five-minute drive to McConnell Air Force Base.

Characteristically, David did kiss me goodbye. He did not say, "I love you." That just wasn't David.

"Write to me as soon as you get there," I reminded him as he walked out the front door of our house. "Let me know when you arrive."

From the front door David walked diagonally across the lawn to the left where the car was waiting for him.

Captain Hrdlicka was wearing his flight suit, a slender flight cap and carrying an olive drab medium-sized duffle bag. It was very early in the morning, and the kids were still sleeping. As I watched my husband angle across the lawn toward the car, I stood at the front door in my pajamas with my hair in curlers. I didn't take my eyes off David. As he approached the car, I heard a voice, "*You will never see him again.*"

As the door to the sedan slammed shut, my heart sank. The car pulled away and out of sight. I stepped back into the house, panic-stricken. I tried to reason with myself, knowing full well how much of a worrywart I've always been, but also a realist. I tried to consider all the possibilities that could occur, so no matter what happened, I would not react as an incapacitated victim. Then, I could handle what came my way, hopefully.

CHAPTER 10

Hickam Air Force Base, Oahu Hawaii, 1965

David and his squadron flew from McConnell AFB in Wichita as a group to Hickam Field in Honolulu, Hawaii. On the layover, the pilots gathered on the lawn near the swimming pool for a Mai Tai drinking contact. The junior officer of the group, Lieutenant Larry Lighty was designated to be the wake-up officer the following morning. His job was to make sure that a hungover group of fighter pilots could get out of bed and into their planes. The club at Hickam was bringing them pitcher after pitcher of Mai Tais. They all had a fun time. After rolling out of bed the next morning, Lighty did his duty. David had one bad hangover, but they all made it airborne the next day.

They flew from Hickam to Guam, then from Guam to the Philippines...he thinks.

Takhli Air Base, Thailand, April 1965

It took two eight-hour flights and one six-hour flight to get to Takhli, Thailand. David and the rest of the 563rd arrived at Takhli and found that the base had not changed much since its occupation by the Japanese during World War II. Basically, a runway with huts that they called "hooches," GI lingo throughout the Orient, probably derived from "uchi," the Japanese word for "house." Hooches were designed for 16 men, but upon arrival, the pilots immediately threw six beds out to give themselves more space. One thing the pilots had to look forward to at Takhli was the officer's club. At Takhli, it was a hooch set aside for partying. Like the rest of the hooches on the airfield, it was made of teak. Everything was made of teak. The timbers were then hand-sewn together. The "Pack Six" nearby on the base sold beer and liquor. But there were rules. Only officers could buy booze. Enlisted men could only buy beer. The pilots and other officers would buy their favorite beverages and then bring it over to the officer's club. They would then write their names on their own bottles. While David participated, he wasn't a heavy drinker. He was more likely to be found attending daily Catholic Mass at Takhli than in the officer's club.

But David was competitive in sports and games, and at Takhli there wasn't much to do but drink and fly missions. But they did have checkers, and according to his fellow pilots, David was a hell of a checker player!

Lighty was from Portland, Oregon. Like David, he had not gone to college, getting his commission through the aviation cadet program. Lighty flew several missions with David and described him as "a strong, funny, and clever man. A great pilot."

Lt. Robert Peel, a Tennessean, was there. He was in the command post at Takhli working on "Frags" or telegram messages that would describe missions and targets to the pilots. But he was trained in the 105 and eventually returned to his pilot duty. Some of the other pilots present at Takhli were Robert Wistrand, Robert Greskowiak, Victor Cole, Sam Woodworth, and Robert C. Miller.

Most of the pilots thought the F-105 was a magnificent flying machine. It had some challenging qualities but some good ones, too. It was a big plane that was hard to shoot down. The cockpit was comparatively spacious, which allowed some bigger guys, well over 6 feet and 200 pounds – unusual for a fighter pilot – to fly the aircraft. But it wasn't very maneuverable and despite good speed, it wasn't very quick; still it was one of the first Mach 2 fighters.

"It was a beast," remembers Larry Lighty, "In order to remove the gear pin, I had to stand on the ground." This was something he would do before he took off.

The F-105 was the fastest fighter we had in the Vietnam War. After hitting their targets, the pilots would push the throttle all the way forward. One pilot said, "I would rock my body like a kid trying to get a little more out of a soap box derby racer. Low level in that hot moist air, the condensation would form around the canopy around your head, and it was like I was hiding from the SAMS and the anti-aircraft guns as I accelerated to more than 1,000 mph."

Memo from David to Carol written from Thailand Base before May

We are about 80 miles north of Bangkok if you care to look it up on a map. In just a few weeks I have seen a jungle menagerie of tigers, elephants, cobra, Russel vipers, not to mention every conceivable bug in the world. We live in what the natives call a hooch. Tin roof, screen louvered sides and bamboo shutters for the hard rains. We sleep under mosquito nets and 85 degrees is about as cool as it gets at night. I had to leave in a hurry, so I borrowed enough money for you to operate on. It looks now as if I might get home sometime in August. It depends on the President. I know you should be moving into our new house this month. I hated to leave you with all the moving. But now is when it pays to have a good wife. I have been pretty blessed along those lines.

Got myself into a little shooting war over here. Things have been straightened out a bit, and I have more time to think now than the first couple weeks we were here.

The following letter was sent to the Grahams who were our tenants on the ranch:

By May 4th Hrdlicka had flown ten combat missions. For Hrdlicka, sometimes they were very intense, and then sometimes they were what he called "milkruns."

Hrdlicka: "We have lost one pilot so far and two planes. Three planes have been hit. Carol, of course, doesn't know, but I got hit last week. Ground fire entered the bottom of my fighter about four feet behind my seat. The shell was a .50 caliber and it cut some hydraulic lines. It hit a real tough spot in the bottom of the plane which slowed it up enough that it glanced off the side of my belly tank. The slug was still in the plane, so I have it as a keepsake. Am getting more used to the heat now, and I don't have to drink as much water anymore. The new pilots who come in really sweat.

"Carol is in our new house now, and the way things are going, we may have an overseas mission before I have a chance to live in it. Sure hope that we go to Germany rather than come back over here. This really is a stupid war.

"We have a fulltime priest now, Father McMillen, and I go to daily Mass with him. I'm not flying today. The Father climbed up the side of my plane as I was standing and gave me his blessing. There are all kinds of motives behind the reason that pilots are here, and I suppose that you know most of this, Jim. There are the groups who think that this isn't much of a war, but it is the best one we have, so they want to be in it. There are groups who want glory. They seem to be people who just have no regard for human life, as long as it isn't their own.

For myself, I think that I hate this war and war in general, but we just can't let a lot of good people go down the tube to Communism. To many people this is fun, but to me, it's just plain hard. You divide my 10 missions by the $55,000 they pay me extra for combat pay, and it comes to about $5 a crack. Not really overpayment, would you say? I thank God that I am lucky enough to have you folks and Al on the place.

* * *

"In May, the target list expanded to include several ammunition storage areas and the 563rd suffered three more losses. On May 9th, Captain Robert Wistrand, 34, from New York, N.Y. was hit by ground fire while attacking an anti-aircraft battery in Laos' Mu Gia Pass. He did not eject. During the mission, Wistrand's aircraft crashed. Wingman observed no parachute and heard no emergency radio beeper signals. Searches of the loss area proved to be fruitless.

"Six days later, Captain Robert Greskowiak, 30, a husband and father of three children from West Allis, Wisconsin died when his Thunderchief lost power on take-off. His ejection seat also failed and Greskowiak crashed at the end of Takhli's runway killing five civilians and wrecking a Buddhist temple.

"Lighty says...'They were both great pilots.'

"The last of four F-105D Thunderchiefs lifted off from the runway at Takhli Air Force Base and climbed to join three others in formation."

CHAPTER 11

Back in Wichita, KS, USA

I worried daily after David departed. I knew David was heading into something that was life-threatening, simply by his being a fighter pilot. Though I cried every night alone when the kids were sleeping, I never showed emotion to others in public or to the children. I generally kept to myself.

I could never fool David playing the stiff upper lip. His favorite saying to me was, "No sweat, I'll handle it, Calm down." *Now, I must be brave for David and the children – for my family.* So I busied myself with the move. Each day I would take the kids to school, then go to work packing. I tried to lose myself in picking out wallpaper and paint for the new house. If ever I needed a project on which to concentrate, it was now.

Once ready to move in, I packed the family's white 1964 Buick station wagon, loading in all the kids' clothes, knick-knacks, and whatever else I could carry and ferried it over to the new house. I moved everything I could by myself. Then, when just the furniture was left, I called the movers.

Naturally, the whole time, David was on my mind. We wrote letters back and forth. I tried to keep my letters light-hearted, trying not to complain if I felt I had my hands full with the house, moving, and the kids. I would simply tell him what the kids were up to. I knew my worries played on my health and appearance but just hoped the kids didn't notice. I had no appetite, and I couldn't sleep.

CHAPTER 12

David Takes the Lead on Mission

May 18th, 1965

It was estimated by U.S. Intelligence analysts that during 1965, 4,500 PAVN (People's Army of Vietnam) troops were infiltrated through Laos along with 300 tons of material each month. The increasing use of Laos to both protect the movement of troops and supplies to the Viet Cong, meant an increase in strikes against targets in Laos. In the early morning hours of May 18th, 1965, David and three other pilots were tasked to attack and bomb portions of rail/road.

After their briefing, the pilots figured that they were going on an easy mission. The target was defined well. Each aircraft carried either six or eight 750-pound bombs. Larry Lighty was flying as David's wingman. Flying down what they called the chute, David was leading. The pilots brought together for the mission were Major Robert C. Miller from Hayward, California, Major Victor Cole, Lieutenant Larry Lighty of Portland, Oregon, and Captain David Hrdlicka of Littleton, Colorado – all trained U.S. Air Force bomber fighter pilots – the best available for the U.S. government's "task at hand," a secret war, for which the selected best pilots the U.S. government had to offer, were deployed. But did the pilots know they were being used in a secret war?

Hrdlicka was not generally a member of Lighty's group. The command staff made up the sorties the night before, setting up who would fly and with whom and when they'd rendezvous with tankers. Flight assignments varied week to week. The decisions were made by the 2nd Air Division in Saigon. Decisions were not being made at Takhli. There were about 25 F-105's on the ground at Takhli at the time.

Captain Hrdlicka flew the lead position under the call sign Plymouth 41. Major Cole flew number two, followed by Major Miller and Lieutenant Lighty. Their mission was to crater and segment a road near Sam Neua, Laos. The four silver aircraft climbed to about 20,000 feet and cruised the hours until they entered Laos and focused on their target.

When they arrived in the target area, they found it was obscured by clouds. They had been warned during their mission brief that day about intense ground fire and flak in the area. They decided to circle the area at higher altitude to allow the clouds to drift away. After circling for 15 or 20 minutes, the clouds cleared. Captain Hrdlicka could see the road now that they were tasked to destroy. Flying from east to west and parallel to the road, Hrdlicka announced he was starting his dive.

"Plymouth 41...rolling in," Hrdlicka called.

He pushed the Thud into a 30-degree dive, Major Cole following right behind. Hrdlicka released his bombs and pulled up, steering his aircraft to the right, now heading south. As Major Cole continued his dive, he watched Hrdlicka's bombs explode on the road, right on target. Cole was still diving at 5,000 feet and then released his payload. R.C. Miller followed Cole, also releasing his payload. As he pulled his Thud out of the dive, Hrdlicka saw his red fire warning lights on his instrument panel suddenly illuminate.

"I've got a fire warning light," Hrdlicka transmitted.

Lighty looked over at the lead aircraft. Fire was emanating from the fuselage. Before he could confirm, Victor Cole's voice came over the radio.

"Flight lead, you're on fire," Cole replied.

Hearing this, Hrdlicka did not delay. He reached down on the sides of his seat and grabbed hold of the handrails. He pulled them up with both hands, the action releasing the glass canopy of the aircraft. He then squeezed their trigger on the handrail, firing him straight up and out of the aircraft at about 10,000 feet. The so-called "butt-flipper/flapper" then jettisoned him out of the seat, his chute opening at the same time.

Lighty looked over and saw Hrdlicka eject. *Oh, Jesus, why did he bail so early?* Lighty thought. Part of their training taught them that if they were hit, to fly as far as they could away from their target area, as that area would obviously be home to the enemy. In Laos, even getting over a ridge to a different village area could be the difference between friend or enemy. Hrdlicka's chute opened and he started drifting slowly toward the ground. Cole turned his aircraft in the direction where Hrdlicka was drifting downward.

"Plymouth 42...I'll watch the chute."

"Roger, 42, I've got the plane," Miller responded, indicating he would follow the path of the now pilotless aircraft. Miller watched the plane descend and crash into the side of a mountain, exploding in a fireball.

From about a half mile away, Cole watched as Hrdlicka hit the ground in a clearing, not far from a village. Cole continued to close on the location but was suddenly under attack by intense flak. Cole climbed above nine thousand feet and started circling the area where Hrdlicka was now on the ground. He desperately looked to see if there was any movement on the ground by Hrdlicka but could not see any. While Cole circled at 9,000 feet, Lighty and Miller circled in their aircraft high above. After about 15 minutes of circling and dodging sporadic flak, Cole could see the parachute being folded up on the ground.

"I'm going down for a look," Cole announced over the radio.

"Roger that," Miller responded, "I'll cover you."

Cole then dove to a lower altitude to get a better look. Flying over Hrdlicka at just 50 feet off the ground, Cole looked to his right and caught a fleeting look of six to eight people in dark clothing who were looking right back at him. One had the parachute under his arm. One was taller than the rest and appeared dressed in a flight suit but had his back to Cole's viewpoint. The others appeared to have surrounded the tallest one. Cole could not tell if they were supporting him upright, or if he was standing under his own power. Cole could not confirm that the person in the middle was Hrdlicka but knew in his heart it was. He noticed no weapons in the group as he flew by. But the scene was enough for him to draw a conclusion.

"The bad guys got him," Cole reported.

Major Cole quickly pulled up, the engines roaring. He climbed back to over 9,000 feet to escape the flak. Turning back, he watched the group of people walking, enter the village and disappear. The three aircraft continued to circle, the pilots watching for further movement, but they were running low on fuel and it was difficult to see any activity from more than 9,000 feet. When they reached the point of having only enough fuel to reach the tanker they left, they rendezvoused with the tanker, and then headed back to Takhli. Cole then returned to the scene of the bailout. This time he noticed two helicopters and four T-28 aircraft working on what they called a pilot pickup. Seeing that they likely didn't know where Hrdlicka had landed, Cole dove and made a low pass over the village where the group had disappeared to show the rescue pilots where the group went. The T-28's circled the area at very low altitude but reported seeing no sign of life in the village. One of the helicopters reported landing at a friendly village just a few miles away. They picked up some of the villagers and flew them to the village where Hrdlicka had landed. The Laotians told the rescue team that it was an enemy village. Cole then left the area. He reported that Hrdlicka had been carrying an emergency radio beacon but said at no time did he hear it transmitting. A total of 21 sorties involving fighters, a tanker, search and rescue aircraft and helicopters were flown in the effort to find and recover Hrdlicka. But Cole, Lighty, and Miller knew full well that Captain David Hrdlicka was now likely in the hands of the Pathet Lao.

CHAPTER 13

Air Force says, 'Don't Worry, It's Not That Bad?'

"Oh my God, I've got to go!" I said to my friend Dot on the other end of the line, as I saw a military car pull up in front of the house and park. I looked down at myself and realized I was still in my pajamas. I ran back to the bedroom to change. The men in the car were now walking up the front yard. I wasn't able to think clearly enough to know what to change into. I finally grabbed a turquoise robe. I knew the dangers of my husband's job. *It was similar,* I reflected, *to being the wife of a police officer or firefighter. I knew the possibility that each time David walked out the door he might not be coming back.*

The doorbell rang. I walked to the door with a growing sense of fear. I opened the door. It was Colonel Carlos Dannacher, the Vice Commander of David's fighter wing, with a chaplain. I did my best to read their faces but came up with nothing. *Military faces,* I thought. The duo moved toward me. I backpedaled, shaking my head side to side, fearing the worst. Seeing my reaction, one of them spoke.

"Oh, it's not that bad. It's not that bad."

I was well aware that David's squadron had already lost one pilot who had been killed in the first few days of their deployment and that another had gone missing a couple of weeks later. I motioned them in and over to the living room where they sat down. They got to the point right away and explained that David had been shot down, that he had bailed out and survived. They told me that he had been surrounded by people on the ground.

"Did he walk away?" I asked.

I wanted to know if he was physically okay. David had a bad back, and I felt he couldn't take being ejected out of his aircraft without doing further damage to his back. I thought the force of the ejection could leave him paralyzed from the waist down. They told me they didn't know if David walked off on his own power or whether he'd been carried away. They told me that he had been taken to a schoolhouse to be interrogated. **They did not tell me that the crash had occurred in Laos.** But they explained to me that in the area where he crashed there were both friendly and non-friendly villages. They told me that a search and rescue helicopter landed at a nearby friendly village where they learned he'd been captured and taken to a schoolhouse to be interrogated by the Pathet Lao.

I felt that they were giving me the best possible scenario and might even be sugarcoating the details. A "schoolhouse" sounded pretty innocent as a place for interrogation by the Pathet Lao.

"Be upfront with me. Give me the facts as they exist."

"We will," Colonel Dannacher assured me.

"You let me make up my mind as to how I want to deal with it," I continued. "Don't tell me any lies. I better not be told any lies...I don't care what the reason."

I knew they felt that wives needed to be handled delicately. Bringing a chaplain along adds a certain delicacy to the touch.

I wanted them to understand that I was not like the other wives in that manner. I assured them that they could talk frankly and directly with me, that it would work better for everyone concerned if they did.

They assured me they would be open and above-board with me, and if they didn't know the answer to a question I had, that they would simply say so. And if they heard anything new about David's condition, they would let me know immediately. After about 20 minutes, they left. Their current military obligation had been completed, informing the wife or family of the death or capture of a military member.

I got back on the phone and called Dot Middlebrooks back. I relayed the information to her, then told her that I had to go and start getting ready. I knew what was coming. An influx of visitors and well-wishers would soon be showing up at the house, and I needed to be ready for them. I got dressed, but I felt automated...in a daze. Looking back on that day, I knew I had to have been in shock. But then I've always tried not to show my emotions in public. All I could think about was David in the hands of the enemy. He would want me to be strong for him and the children. I told myself that I had to function, no matter how anguished I felt.

Around noon, people started arriving at the house. I was aware that I still felt in a fog. There were people coming and going, and the small house was always full to capacity in the following hours. I began to realize that I was very tired....

I realized that for many women it might be comforting to have the support of the Air Force community and the wives of other pilots, but I also knew I was not hardwired that way. While I was grateful for their gestures, I preferred to be left alone. I think perhaps the Air Force should consider the wife's preferences and maybe even ask her.

I wanted to think about David and try to connect with him, no matter his condition. I know that loved ones can intuit each other's thoughts and condition. How many times has it been documented that when the phone rings during the night that a wife, husband, or parent knows well before answering the loved one what the phone call is about! I didn't feel this yet. I felt David was still alive. But with that hopeful feeling, I did want to cry, to scream, to beat against fate for this turn of events. I just didn't want to show my own vulnerabilities to others.

For now, I kept filling cups of coffee, thanking people for their support, and playing hostess. I was amazed at how long people lingered. It's insane! I don't think that some ever question what they are there for. It's so easy for even a death to turn into a wake, an excuse for a social gathering with little consideration given to the individual for whom the protocoled gathering is taking place – whether she wanted it!

A couple of hours into having company, my son David Jr. arrived home from school. I immediately took him to the back of the house and into the master bedroom. I looked into my son's eyes, his father's eyes, and gave him the news directly and as courageously as I could for his sake.

"Your Dad was shot down. The bad guys got him, but he's coming home when the whole thing is over."

The seven-year-old David Jr. was processing this. What he heard was...that his Dad was eventually coming home. He took the bad news with a sense of hope.

"Son, if you're going to cry, cry now," but at the same time, I realized that I was ordering him to cry on demand, or else don't cry. I know I wanted to cry so badly myself that I suppose I was projecting my wishes onto my son.

David Jr. didn't shed a tear...that I know of. I want to think that he heard **hope** in what was without doubt a shocking revelation concerning his beloved Dad. *I don't expect him to have the stoic attitude of an adult at seven years of age, nor do I ex-*

pect a seven-year-old boy to be capable of comforting his grieving mom; that would certainly dispel any hope he had. I only know that I am done with feeling responsible and obligated right now. I want to turn inward.

Even when everyone left, I had three little children to take care of. I didn't tell the two youngest. They would not understand. I needed to keep their life as normal as possible. I held myself together until I could be alone. Once I put them to bed, I finally had a moment to sit down. That is when the magnitude of what I was told hit me with unrelenting force. I went into my bedroom, closed the door, and smothered my sobs face-down into a pillow.

David's family after shoot down

CHAPTER 14

It's Far Worse

How am I going to deal with all this? I felt like a hamster running in a cage. I couldn't sleep, I couldn't eat...I just had to keep running on the treadmill going nowhere. That is the agony. There was absolutely nothing I could do to help the man I loved. Not having any control over the situation that could determine a loved one's fate is the worst sort of situation that anyone could ever live through. There is no comfort to be had from anyone anywhere. I had to accept that for now. I trusted that the Air Force looked out for its own and felt that they would do everything possible to rescue David. He would be home soon.

I did anything to stay busy. After trying to go to bed, I couldn't sleep. I would get up and pace the floor. After the kids left for school, I did chores to keep myself busy. I cleaned the house and then cleaned it again and again. Thoughts raced through my mind. I didn't know how to confront my grief.

I would hear David's voice, "*Don't worry about that. I'll take care of it when I come home.*"

* * *

I felt the frustration of trying to cope with not knowing David's fate, feeling that I had been told the bare minimum. At times, I felt so much anger, I frightened even myself. I was careful never to reveal my feelings to the children. It would have taken an outsider who knew me before to really know how this was changing me. The change was not going to be for the better, at least in the eyes of others. I wanted answers from those responsible for my husband's welfare....and that was the United States Air Force. The Air Force has departments that handle this sort of thing, or at least claim to. The only problem is, Casualty Assistance has no idea how to deal with what they're assigned to do! They weren't even trying to be helpful.

"What information do you have for me on Captain Hrdlicka? What's being done to find him? Where, precisely, is he being held prisoner of war? Who's in charge there? What do you mean you can't tell me anything?! You will tell me!" I screamed into the receiver.

To Head of Casualty, "Mrs. Hrdlicka called again today, yelling again."

But I wanted to know, what is so hard to understand about keeping a wife informed as to developments involving her husband being held as a prisoner of war? David was in the hands of the enemy. The Air Force had informed me of only that much...then silence...nothing.

They might as well have said, "It's your problem if he's being tortured and you can't deal with it. Deal with it! You knew from the beginning that you were an Air Force fighter pilot's wife."

I don't know why the Air Force doesn't just give the wife of a fighter pilot a release to sign that she will not cause any problem by questioning the Air Force about updates on her husband once he is announced as a POW, once he has served his purpose for the Air Force. I spent my days and nights crying when I wasn't justifiably screaming into the phone at the Casualty Team. If a loved one could very well be undergoing daily torture by the enemy, what would you say your obligation to telling the wife is?

I made it my business to be aware of what that torture meant specifically. Are they breaking David's fingers? Are they pulling his fingernails out? Oh, yes, I was very up to date on all the latest North Vietnam war torture. Because I read everything that I could get my hands on regarding the Vietnam War from as many different sources as I could, I was well-informed, despite the efforts of the U.S. Air Force not to disclose the facts to families of POW and MIA victims.

Naively, I originally believed that because David had been shot down in Laos, he had a better chance of getting out and returning home sooner. Several people had assured me that the Laotians were not as vicious as the North Vietnamese. Though this, at first, gave me comfort, my frustration, sense of helplessness, and mounting anger returned. Some people will just tell you whatever they think will allow you to gain some solace, some peace. I do not know the person who can gain solace under such circumstances. It's certainly not me. I devoured every source of information from abroad, from any country I could, to educate myself, to develop what I considered to be a valid worldview, and especially on the Vietnam War, the war that had taken my closest loved one from me. Every country, including our dear old U.S. of A. has its war propaganda. If U.S. citizens aren't aware of that, they're being hoodwinked to the nth degree.

CHAPTER 15

Pilots Base in Thailand

Takhli Royal Air Force Base, Thailand

Before David was shot down, the crew chief would meet the pilots with a beer. They would then head to the debriefing shack to talk about what they did right and what they could have done better on their missions. After David was shot down, they debriefed each pilot individually.

Miller and Cole were more experienced than Lighty. These are the same pilots who accompanied David the day his plane was shot down. At this point, Lighty was probably up to 25 or 30 missions. Lighty thought he was first to accomplish 60 missions. 100 missions, and you were on your way home.

The guys at Tahkli tracked any news they could on Hrdlicka. But for those who served with, lived with, and knew David, trying to keep track of what was going on was a continuous horror story. They heard he was being held in a cave, then heard he was being kept near the border of Laos and North Vietnam. Rumors circulated that he was being kept in a pen or cage. They heard other stories of attempts to rescue and free Hrdlicka. But the stories never seemed to come to fruition. They also heard the warning that any attempt to free him would result in his death. For the pilots still serving at

Takhli, David remained on their minds and in their hearts. After their four-month tour, Lighty and many others were sent home.

Hickam Air Force Base Honolulu, Hawaii, 1965

David Hrdlicka's former wingman Bob Dornan walked through the Casualty Center at the base. He had heard of a few F-105 shootdowns and wanted to see if he recognized any names. The Air Force had just set up an organization to track POWs and MIAs.

"Can you show me the list of POWs and MIAs?" Dornan requested.

The airman on duty handed over the docket. As Dornan looked down, the first name he saw was his friend, David Hrdlicka.

"Oh my God, they've got David!"

Dornan continued to browse the pages in front of him, but his mind and heart were on his friend.

"Is he in Hanoi?" asked Dornan.

"No, he's in Laos somewhere," said the airman.

Dornan felt much guilt over the fact that many of the guys he had served with were killed or had become POWs in Vietnam after he got out of the Air Force.

CHAPTER 16

U.S. Presidential Defense for Being in Vietnam

July 28, 1965

As I struggled to make sense of what was going on with my husband, Americans were struggling to make sense of why the United States was getting involved in a small jungle nation more than eight thousand miles away. In July of 1965, President Johnson addressed the American people to give his explanation as to why America had entered Southeast Asia and Vietnam.

> This is a different kind of war. There are no marching armies or solemn declarations. Some citizens of South Viet-Nam at times, with understandable grievances, have joined in the attack on their own government.
>
> First, we intend to convince the Communists that we cannot be defeated by force of arms or by superior power. They are not easily convinced. In recent months they have greatly increased their fighting forces and their attacks and the number of incidents.
>
> I have asked the Commanding General, General Westmoreland, what more he needs to meet the mounting aggression. He has told me. We will meet his needs.

I have today ordered to Viet-Nam the Air Mobile Division and certain other forces by raising the monthly draft call from 17,000 over a period of time to 35,000 per month, and for us to step up our campaign for voluntary enlistments.

After this past week of deliberations, I have concluded that it is not essential to order Reserve units into service now. If that necessity should later be indicated, I will give the matter more careful consideration and I will give the country – you – an adequate notice before taking such action, but only after full preparations.

We have also discussed with the Government of South Vietnam lately, the steps that we will take to substantially increase their own effort, both on the battlefield and toward reform and progress in the villages. Ambassador Lodge is now formulating a new program to be tested upon his return to that area.

I have directed Secretary Rusk and Secretary McNamara to be available immediately to the Congress to review with these committees, the appropriate congressional committees, what we plan to do in these areas. I have asked them to be able to answer the questions of any Member of Congress.

Secretary McNamara, in addition, will ask the Senate Appropriations Committee to add a limited amount to present legislation to help meet part of this new cost until a supplemental measure is ready and hearings can be held when the Congress assembles in January. In the meantime, we must not let this mask the central fact that this is really war. It is guided by North Viet-Nam and it is spurred by Communist China. Its goal is to conquer the South, to defeat American power, and to extend the Asiatic dominion of Communism. There are great stakes in the balance. Most of the non-Communist nations of Asia cannot, by themselves and alone, resist the growing might and the grasping ambition of Asian Communism.

Our power, therefore, is a very vital shield. If we are driven from the field in Viet-Nam, then no nation can ever again have the same confidence in American promise, or in American protection.

In each land the forces of independence would be considerably weakened, and an Asia so threatened by Communist domination would certainly imperil the security of the United States itself.

We did not choose to be the guardians at the gate, but there is no one else.

Nor would surrender in Viet-Nam bring peace, because we learned from Hitler at Munich that success only feeds the appetite of aggression. The battle would be renewed in one country and then another country, bringing with it perhaps even larger and crueler conflict, as we have learned from the lessons of history.

Moreover, we are in Viet-Nam to fulfill one of the most solemn pledges of the American Nation. Three Presidents – President Eisenhower, President Kennedy, and your present President – over 11 years have committed themselves and have promised to help defend this small and valiant nation.

Strengthened by that promise, the people of South Viet-Nam have fought for many long years. Thousands of them have died. Thousands more have been crippled and scarred by war. We just cannot now dishonor our word, or abandon our commitment, or leave those who believed us and who trusted us to the terror and repression and murder that would follow.

This, then, my fellow Americans, is why we are in Viet-Nam.

CHAPTER 17

Photo of David's Capture

July 22, 1966

The Vietnamese newspaper, *Quan Nhan Dan,* featured a story on David's capture. My father-in-law called to tell me that the article contained a picture of David in custody shortly after his shoot down. I immediately hung up and called Casualty and demanded they get me a copy of that article and picture.

When the picture arrived by mail it brought me great relief. It showed David alive on the ground in his flight suit being taken into custody just after his shootdown. *Thank God he is walking,* I thought. To me, David looked well, not in any pain. I had been of the assumption that David may have been severely injured when he ejected from the plane. The picture showed David walking! That gave me great hope. He was in good shape and would be able to survive his ordeal in captivity.

I learned that the article was the work of the Russian newspaper, *Pravda.* It eventually showed up in the *Denver Post.* Hanoi publication *Quan Doi Nhan Dan* printed a capture photo which then made the rounds appearing in *Pravda.*

Months later my father-in-law called again, and we talked about David's situation and what might likely be happening in that cave over in Laos.

"David's probably not being tortured anymore because there would be nothing to tell them at this point," said David's father.

Hearing him say that was jarring, but at the same time somewhat comforting as it made me hopeful that there would be no torture.

Vientiane, Laos, July 26, 1966

The radio crackled. The voice was not familiar to any who were listening. The words were slow and deliberate. They were spoken without feeling. But across the Pathet Lao stronghold the message was clear. The Pathet Lao had an American pilot in custody, and that pilot was a powerful piece of propaganda. The recording had been made in a cave near Sam Neua, Laos, and was being broadcast across much of the country, Vietnam, and was even picked up by Radio Peking in China.

> When I piloted a plane on a bombing mission, I was unable to see the contradictions in realities. The Johnson Administration lied to me, saying that I was sent to bomb the communication lines from Northern to Southern Laos. This proves that the U.S. Imperialists have deliberately invaded Laos by force. I see that the Laotian problem must be solved peacefully by the Laotians themselves without U.S. intervention and aggression, and that this settlement must be based strictly on the Articles of the 1952 Geneva Agreements. It was mentioned that the United States would not be authorized to send officers and soldiers to Laos, and that the United States and Thailand would not be allowed to use that territory as a military base for aggression in Laos. However, these two countries have attacked the liberated areas of the patriotic forces. Now, as I write this letter to your Highness requesting my release, flying above me there are U.S. jets coming to bomb. Your

Highness, if you will send me back to rejoin my small family, I will never forget your good will. My small family will open its door to welcome your Highness and people with sincerity at any time. Once again, I beg your Highness to pardon me and to release me so that I will be able to rejoin my children and my family. I will guide my comrades in the struggle to voice protests against the government, which is cruelly, savagely, and inhumanely invading Laos.

With my sincere wishes,

Capt. David L. Hrdlicka of the U.S. Armed Forces in Thailand

* * *

January 7, 1967

In what is still a heavily classified operation, General Richard Secord directed the only successful prisoner-of-war rescue of the Vietnam War. During the Ban Naden raid a team of the CIA's hill-tribe mercenaries was inserted out of hearing of the POW prison; their surprise raid quickly wiped out about 40 guards. It was then discovered there were twice as many prisoners as expected. Nine Air America (CIA) H-34 helicopters dropped into the middle of the Ho Chi Minh Trail and rescued 53 Asian prisoners. This rescue is still used as a case study in CIA training for covert operations. Was there hope that David might be rescued in a similar operation? That was already being planned, and Secord was involved.

May 5, 1967

A Laotian representative advised the International Committee of the Red Cross in Geneva, Switzerland, that Hrdlicka had been captured.

1969

I am told by Air Force Casualty that David died as a prisoner-of-war, yet they were never able to provide any specifics or evidence surrounding the claim. Ivan Shchedrov, a Russian writer who wrote many articles on Laos, states that he saw David in 1969. I was then communicating with Colonel A. W. Gratch who called and told me, "A POW in Laos was shot. We don't know if it was David or Shelton." The next time he called and told me, "A POW has died from dysentery...we don't know if it was David or Shelton."

They were never able to provide me with any specific evidence proving that David was dead.

CHAPTER 18

Getting on with Life

1970-1971

I felt like I was on a yo-yo. One day I would think that David had died. The next day I'd question that, saying to myself, *I don't have proof that he's dead, so he must be alive.* I was second-guessing myself after the first year, when I firmly believed our government was going to get David out. It was just a question of when. By year two, it became more doubtful, and by the third year, I started collecting myself and believing that I needed to move forward with decisions about what I was going to do with the rest of my life and the lives of my children.

The area of Wichita where I lived with my three children had a huge high school. I thought my son, David, would not get to play sports because he wasn't a big guy. I wanted my children to have an opportunity to play sports at a smaller school, so I moved from Wichita to Rose Hill, Kansas, about 10 miles out of town, in 1971. While a move to a new town and a new home may have felt like starting a new life, it didn't feel like that to me. I did it for the kids, though, giving them more opportunities in a school with much smaller class sizes.

There were still many frustrations that I was dealing with in addition to continual worry about David. Without David's signature, I couldn't sell the house. I needed to find an attorney. But the state of Kansas had just passed a new bill stating that if someone was missing for seven years, he could be declared dead. Therefore, I could basically have David declared dead and could sell the house.

Understandably, I was reluctant to do that, though. Besides the fact that I didn't want to think there was no more hope of David returning, I also thought that it might provide the military with a way to get themselves off the hook, to disavow any further concern for David. I called my casualty assistance officer.

"If I declare David dead in order to sell my house, does that mean that you can use that to declare him dead?"

"Absolutely not," was the response.

If the military could have used that against me, I would not have done it. But feeling secure in knowing I could get the declaration and move, I completed the paperwork, sold the house, and moved just outside of Wichita with the kids.

CHAPTER 19

False Alarm

Fall 1972

In the fall of 1972, National Security Adviser Henry Kissinger told reporters,

"Peace is at hand."

His statement was premature. A tentative agreement between the U.S. and North Vietnam was torpedoed by demands made from South Vietnamese President Nguyen Van Thieu. In the coming weeks, the talks were near collapse and finally deadlocked. President Nixon used the word "impasse," and Kissinger lobbied him to unleash the bombers. During an Oval Office tape recording on December 14, 1972, Kissinger advocated "bombing the bejesus out of them."

Starting December 18, an unprecedented bombing campaign, code-named Linebacker II, was launched against targets around Hanoi and the port of Haiphong. Over the next 12 days, with a 24-hour reprieve on Christmas day, 3,400 sorties were flown over North Vietnam.

The nightly bombardment was costly on both sides.

On the third night, one of the pilots remarked, "I was on my concrete pallet and looking out the window, there was one of those fireballs in the air and a B-52 wing fluttering down."

An analysis of Linebacker II issued by Air University in 1976 made a conservative estimate of 884 SAMs fired at B-52s during the campaign. More than two dozen U.S. aircraft were lost, most of them B-52s. Close to 100 pilots and aircrew were casualties: killed, missing-in-action, or taken as new prisoners.

For the North Vietnamese, the destruction was debilitating. Former POW Larry Spencer described the devastation he saw, while being transferred between prisons:

"There was not a building standing. The B-52s had destroyed the infrastructure and industrial areas of Hanoi."

The Vietnamese made a smart decision in saying, "We're not going to have a country left if we don't get this stopped."

The collateral damage in civilian areas was denounced: a Hanoi-area hospital destroyed, foreign embassies damaged, and residential neighborhoods hit, with estimates of civilian deaths surpassing 2,000. President Nixon was condemned, at home and abroad, but the "Christmas Bombing" of 1972 was a catalyst for compromise. The stalled Paris peace talks reconvened on January 8, 1973, and a final agreement quickly took shape.

Then, on January 27, 1973, almost a half century ago, the final signing ceremony at the Majestic Hotel in Paris was broadcast live across the United States. It was the master plan for ending America's role in the conflict. There was to be a cease-fire, the release of prisoners-of-war, and the parallel withdrawal of U.S. forces within 60 days, as well as a political road map for South Vietnam. Absent from the formalities were the two key figures in the negotiations, Henry Kissinger and Hanoi's senior diplomat, Le Duc Tho. After years of meetings, both in public and in secret, the two were jointly awarded the Nobel Peace Prize in October, which Le Duc Tho declined to accept.

The delegations were seated at a colossal circular table, with two smaller rectangular tables on either side. For the United States, South Vietnam, North Vietnam, and the Provisional Revolutionary Government representing the Viet Cong. The next day's *New York Times* bannered:

"Vietnam Peace Pacts Signed, America's Longest War Halts"

What the public had not been told, and certainly the POW families did not know at the time, was that Kissinger, in addition to the Christmas bombing, had induced the North Vietnamese to sign the peace agreement by secretly agreeing to the North Vietnamese request for substantial reparations. As a guarantee that the U.S. government would honor that promise, the North Vietnamese withheld POWs. Politically, since the appropriation of the money would have required the approval of Congress, it would have been a very difficult promise to honor. When the Watergate scandal came to a head, it became impossible. But since the American public had been told that all the POWs had been returned, the easy way out for the U.S. government was to continue to adhere to that story, whatever contrary facts might come to light in the years ahead.

CHAPTER 20

Lies, Lies, and More Lies

January 1973

"All our American POWs are on their way home," declared President Richard Nixon on TV to the American watching audience of millions across the U.S.

"No, they're not," I said back to the President's face on the television screen. "Who's lying now?"

I felt shock and anger in the moment. The President's announcement made my stomach turn. I had received the call that David was not among the prisoners coming home.

"There's been a little glitch. David's not in the first wave," Casualty told me, offering hope that there were still further waves of prisoners coming home. They told me they were still working on it. Numb to the core by now, I believed them. They told me they would follow up and let me know. But at least they weren't telling me they thought he was dead, as they had done in 1968.

When 591 American POWs all finally came home in 1973, David Hrdlicka was not among them. The Vietnamese claimed that the Pathet Lao had no facilities for holding prisoners, although there is ample evidence to indicate otherwise.

Although Lao publicly stated they held "tens of tens" of American prisoners, the U.S. never negotiated for nearly 600 Americans left in Laos—never released, and never returned. These Americans were not included in Kissinger's Plan of Compromise in the Paris Peace Talks, from which Kissinger was absent. These American POWs were abandoned according to the official Air Force account of the loss of David Hrdlicka, "No information was ever received regarding his fate."

My husband, David Hrdlicka, remains on the rolls of the POWs because "his remains have not been recovered and returned."

Rose Hill, Kansas, 1977

The phone rang. I picked it up and it was Casualty calling.

"Mrs. Hrdlicka, We wanted to let you know that David's official status will soon be changed to 'Died While Captured' on November 21, 1977, having been promoted through the ranks to Colonel during the time he was missing.

"There will be a hearing in Texas. You will be allowed to attend the hearing if you have information that he is still alive. Unless you have any information that David is alive and his whereabouts, they will declare him dead."

"How could I have any information?" I replied, "I don't have access to any of the intelligence. You should have that!"

"We have not heard anything about David, so he will be declared dead at the hearing in Texas. The hearing will be in San Antonio, Texas, at Randolph Air Force Base."

I never saw any documents until the Air Force turned David's file over to me in 1977 after the hearing in Texas when David was officially declared dead. When I looked at the file's documents, stories of David's death were not accurate and contained shootdown dates of other pilots. There was no new evidence presented with the Presumption of Death Declaration. Also, included in the file was a document about a rescue in 1966 falling through.

CHAPTER 21

Coping with Finality

November 21, 1977

I felt as though I had existed in a bubble since I last saw David walk across our yard to get in the military car. The voice I heard—that I would never see my husband again—still haunts me. What do I have left of him? My children and my love for him. That will never change.

I did everything I know possible to stay on top of Casualty to find David. I told his superior the day he and the chaplain came into my house to tell me David had been shot down to be open and above board with me about what they knew. So, when I received the call that they were going to officially declare David dead, and Nixon had said he had brought home all the POWs, I saw no more doors to open. When the Air Force made David's death official, it's like your "father" telling you to get on with your life. The military was akin to a family. I was still young and extremely naïve. I didn't know my rights, what I could do on my own, how far I could have pushed. I did as I was told by the Air Force. I got on with my life, mothering David's three children responsibly. The Declaration of Death at the hearing was the final nail hammered into David's coffin, and the Air Force had done it.

Since David was shot down, most of our military friends had moved on and it became necessary to make new civilian friends. And since I had moved with the kids to Rose Hill, that also precipitated major changes in our life. I have always been toughest on myself, and for me, living with my emotions on my sleeve was never an option. David would expect me to be strong and above all, sensible. I craved having a partner to talk with, to share happy and sad times with, and to share responsibilities. I was so very tired of Herculean efforts to do what needed to be done. There was a popular Eddy Arnold song between the years 1965 to 1977, "Make the World Go Away" ("and get it off of my shoulders"), that expresses perfectly what I had come to feel as my new normal.

The next decade of the 1980s would usher in a new husband for me with a new life to live having a partner to share it with. He was a farmer from Conway Springs, Kansas. We shared similar interests and were compatible. Truth be told, though, David was a ghost in our marriage.

Though frustrated to no end with the Air Force's formal designation of David's death with no proof whatsoever, I just hoped that they might in due time reveal more about what happened to David. No, I was not satisfied with their hearing. In due time, my feelings of the Air Force treating David as a spent cause no longer worthy of attention ignited what was smoldering inside me. I would later come to see that the Air Force had actually tried much harder to declare David dead than to find him.

I would re-emerge on an international stage ready to take on anyone standing in my way in my effort to find out what actually happened to David. The Vietnam War had ended officially in 1973. When the Democratic Republic of Vietnam (DRV) and the Provisional Revolutionary Government (PRG) released their lists of U.S. prisoners to the United States Government on 27 January 1973, none of the names of men known to have been captured in Laos appeared on either list. The absence of any names of U.S. prisoners from Laos on either the DRV or PRG lists was particularly disconcerting, because it was known at the time that a small number of Americans had been captured in Laos, David among them. They were then moved to North Vietnam for detention and were still in North Vietnamese prison camps. So, the U.S. government made no allowance for any POWs possibly remaining in prison camps in Laos. If POWs were not in the group returned home in '73, the U.S. government simply declared them dead.

Part II

CHAPTER 22

Awakening

Conway Springs, Kansas, February 1990

I grabbed my coat as I ventured out to collect the mail. I don't know if it's my age at 52, or just that the winters here in Kansas are frigid, but I don't even go to the mailbox without a coat. Opening the mailbox, I pulled out a letter from the Defense Intelligence Agency (DIA).

When I was inside again and warm, standing in the living room, I carefully opened the envelope, noting that the return address was Washington, D.C. As I read the letter, it stated that David had tried to escape. I was shocked and thought to myself *how does a dead man try to escape?* Then the letter went on to explain how the source was not credible, so once again the agency debunked the report and once again, I believed them.

July 1990

I retrieved a brown envelope from the mailbox postmarked from Washington D.C. There was no accompanying cover letter, so I scanned the document and to my disbelief and astonishment it stated,

"I am talking to General Chaeng suspected of holding David Hrdlicka and friends." The hair on the back of my neck stood up.

"My God! Oh my God! They are speaking in present tense."

I panicked, "What in hell is going on?!" I said aloud to no one.

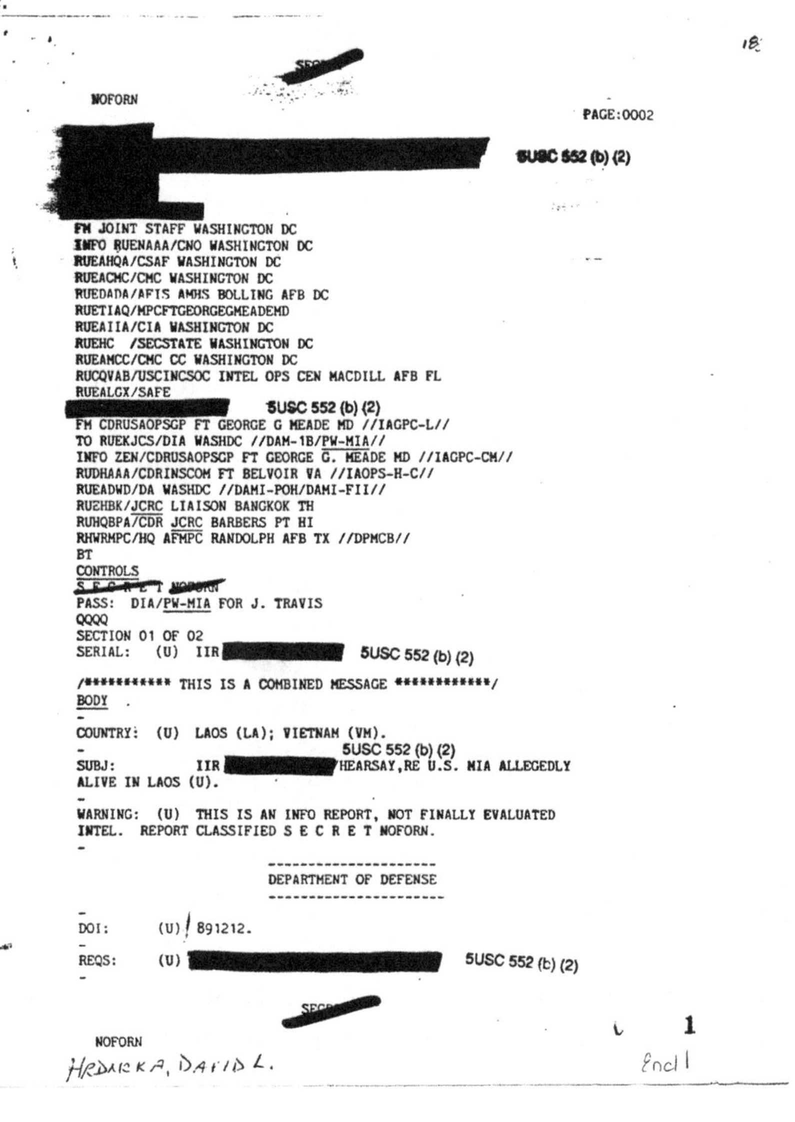

NOFORN

PAGE:0002

5USC 552 (b) (2)

FM JOINT STAFF WASHINGTON DC
INFO RUENAAA/CNO WASHINGTON DC
RUEAHQA/CSAF WASHINGTON DC
RUEACMC/CMC WASHINGTON DC
RUEDADA/AFIS AMHS BOLLING AFB DC
RUETIAQ/MPCFTGEORGEGMEADEMD
RUEAIIA/CIA WASHINGTON DC
RUEHC /SECSTATE WASHINGTON DC
RUEAMCC/CMC CC WASHINGTON DC
RUCQVAB/USCINCSOC INTEL OPS CEN MACDILL AFB FL
RUEALGX/SAFE
5USC 552 (b) (2)
FM CDRUSAOPSGP FT GEORGE G MEADE MD //IAGPC-L//
TO RUEKJCS/DIA WASHDC //DAM-1B/PW-MIA//
INFO ZEN/CDRUSAOPSCP FT GEORGE G. MEADE MD //IAGPC-CM//
RUDHAAA/CDRINSCOM FT BELVOIR VA //IAOPS-H-C//
RUEADWD/DA WASHDC //DAMI-POH/DAMI-FII//
RUEHBK/JCRC LIAISON BANGKOK TH
RUHQBPA/CDR JCRC BARBERS PT HI
RHWRMPC/HQ AFMPC RANDOLPH AFB TX //DPMCB//
BT
CONTROLS
PASS: DIA/PW-MIA FOR J. TRAVIS
QQQQ
SECTION 01 OF 02
SERIAL: (U) IIR 5USC 552 (b) (2)

/*********** THIS IS A COMBINED MESSAGE ************/
BODY

COUNTRY: (U) LAOS (LA); VIETNAM (VM).

SUBJ: IIR 5USC 552 (b) (2) HEARSAY,RE U.S. MIA ALLEGEDLY ALIVE IN LAOS (U).

WARNING: (U) THIS IS AN INFO REPORT, NOT FINALLY EVALUATED INTEL. REPORT CLASSIFIED S E C R E T NOFORN.

DEPARTMENT OF DEFENSE

DOI: (U) 891212.

REQS: (U) 5USC 552 (b) (2)

NOFORN

1

HRDLICKA, DAVID L.

Encl 1

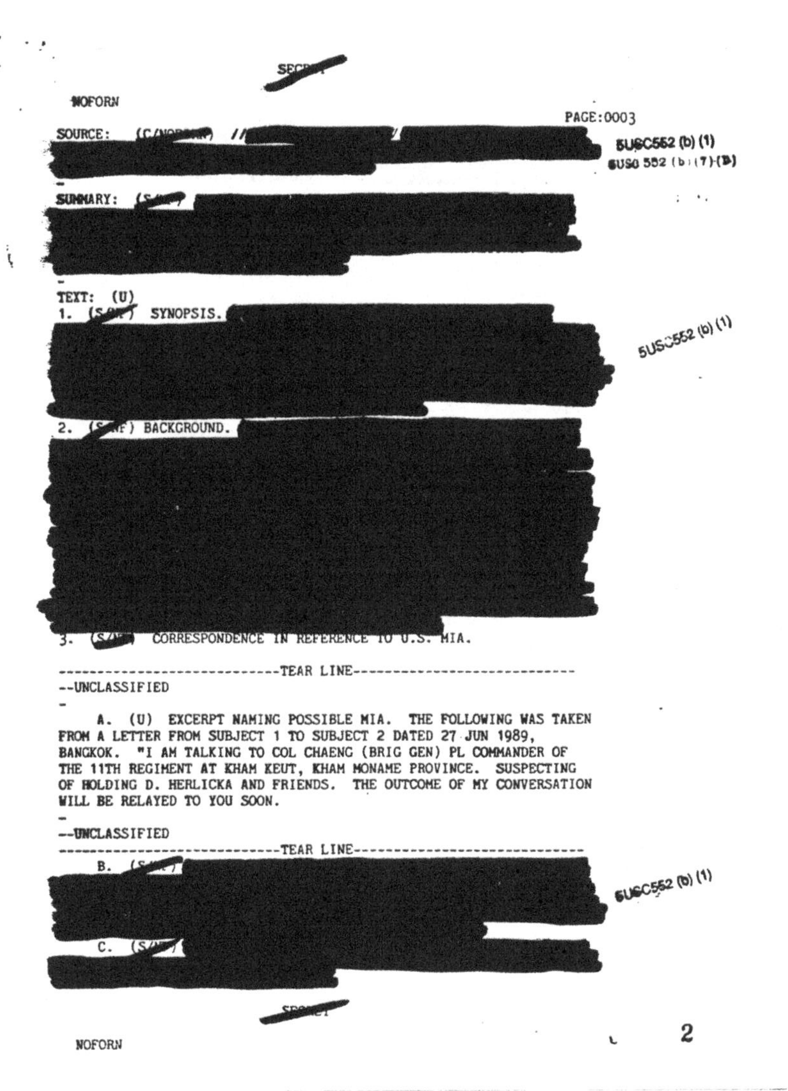
SECRET

NOFORN

PAGE:0003

SOURCE: (C/NOFORN) //

5USC552 (b) (1)
5USC 552 (b)(7)(D)

SUMMARY: (S/NF)

TEXT: (U)
1. (S/NF) SYNOPSIS.

5USC552 (b) (1)

2. (S/NF) BACKGROUND.

3. (S/NF) CORRESPONDENCE IN REFERENCE TO U.S. MIA.

----------------------------TEAR LINE----------------------------
--UNCLASSIFIED
-
A. (U) EXCERPT NAMING POSSIBLE MIA. THE FOLLOWING WAS TAKEN FROM A LETTER FROM SUBJECT 1 TO SUBJECT 2 DATED 27 JUN 1989, BANGKOK. "I AM TALKING TO COL CHAENG (BRIG GEN) PL COMMANDER OF THE 11TH REGIMENT AT KHAM KEUT, KHAM MONAME PROVINCE. SUSPECTING OF HOLDING D. HERLICKA AND FRIENDS. THE OUTCOME OF MY CONVERSATION WILL BE RELAYED TO YOU SOON.
-
--UNCLASSIFIED
----------------------------TEAR LINE----------------------------
B. (S/NF)

5USC552 (b) (1)

C. (S/NF)

SECRET

NOFORN

2

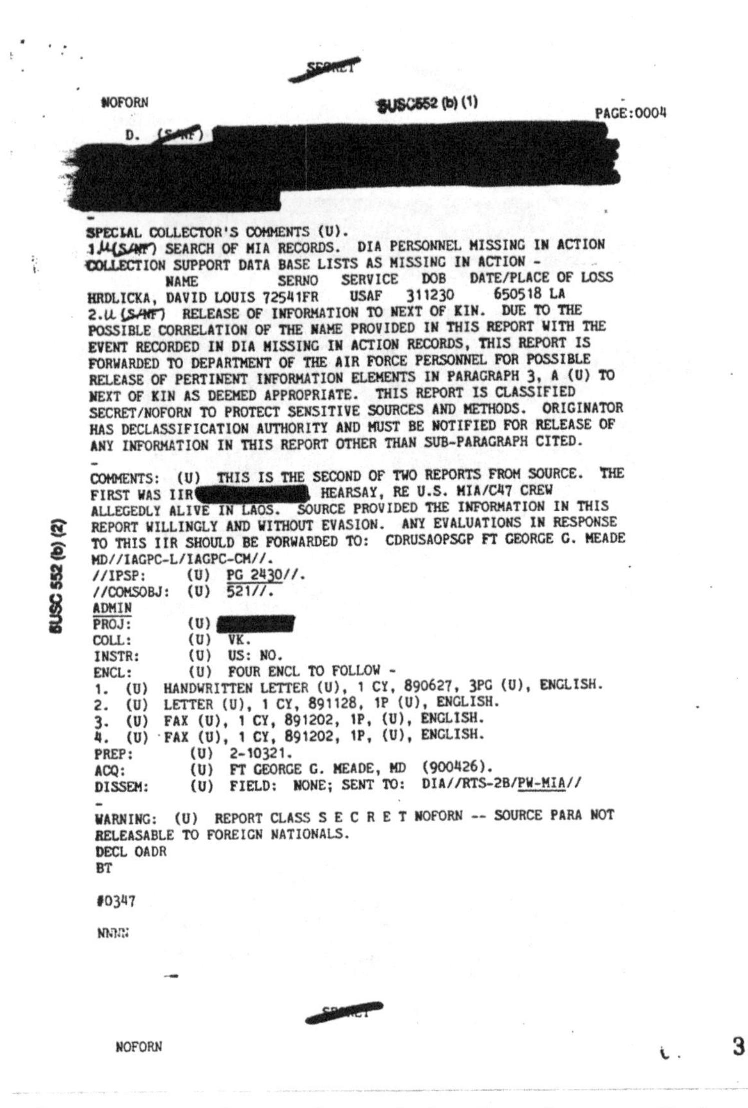

SECRET

NOFORN 5USC552 (b) (1) PAGE:0004

D. (S/NF)

SPECIAL COLLECTOR'S COMMENTS (U).
1.U (S/NF) SEARCH OF MIA RECORDS. DIA PERSONNEL MISSING IN ACTION COLLECTION SUPPORT DATA BASE LISTS AS MISSING IN ACTION -

NAME	SERNO	SERVICE	DOB	DATE/PLACE OF LOSS
HRDLICKA, DAVID LOUIS	72541FR	USAF	311230	650518 LA

2.U (S/NF) RELEASE OF INFORMATION TO NEXT OF KIN. DUE TO THE POSSIBLE CORRELATION OF THE NAME PROVIDED IN THIS REPORT WITH THE EVENT RECORDED IN DIA MISSING IN ACTION RECORDS, THIS REPORT IS FORWARDED TO DEPARTMENT OF THE AIR FORCE PERSONNEL FOR POSSIBLE RELEASE OF PERTINENT INFORMATION ELEMENTS IN PARAGRAPH 3, A (U) TO NEXT OF KIN AS DEEMED APPROPRIATE. THIS REPORT IS CLASSIFIED SECRET/NOFORN TO PROTECT SENSITIVE SOURCES AND METHODS. ORIGINATOR HAS DECLASSIFICATION AUTHORITY AND MUST BE NOTIFIED FOR RELEASE OF ANY INFORMATION IN THIS REPORT OTHER THAN SUB-PARAGRAPH CITED.

COMMENTS: (U) THIS IS THE SECOND OF TWO REPORTS FROM SOURCE. THE FIRST WAS IIR HEARSAY, RE U.S. MIA/C47 CREW ALLEGEDLY ALIVE IN LAOS. SOURCE PROVIDED THE INFORMATION IN THIS REPORT WILLINGLY AND WITHOUT EVASION. ANY EVALUATIONS IN RESPONSE TO THIS IIR SHOULD BE FORWARDED TO: CDRUSAOPSGP FT GEORGE G. MEADE MD//IAGPC-L/IAGPC-CM//.

5USC 552 (b) (2)

//IPSP: (U) PG 2430//.
//COMSOBJ: (U) 521//.
ADMIN
PROJ: (U)
COLL: (U) VK.
INSTR: (U) US: NO.
ENCL: (U) FOUR ENCL TO FOLLOW -
1. (U) HANDWRITTEN LETTER (U), 1 CY, 890627, 3PG (U), ENGLISH.
2. (U) LETTER (U), 1 CY, 891128, 1P (U), ENGLISH.
3. (U) FAX (U), 1 CY, 891202, 1P, (U), ENGLISH.
4. (U) FAX (U), 1 CY, 891202, 1P, (U), ENGLISH.
PREP: (U) 2-10321.
ACQ: (U) FT GEORGE G. MEADE, MD (900426).
DISSEM: (U) FIELD: NONE; SENT TO: DIA//RTS-2B/PW-MIA//

WARNING: (U) REPORT CLASS S E C R E T NOFORN -- SOURCE PARA NOT RELEASABLE TO FOREIGN NATIONALS.
DECL OADR
BT

#0347

NNNN

SECRET

NOFORN 3

What I was reading indicated that David was still alive as recently as a few months ago, a year at most. I felt overwhelmed. I looked back at the envelope. It had come from the DIA, but there was no accompanying letter explaining why it had been sent to me or who was responsible for sending it.

I immediately called the DIA and demanded to know what was going on.

"When you told me that the 1989 escape attempt was a false sighting, I bought your answer. Now I receive this Chaeng report that David *is* alive. You are not giving me all the information on my husband that you have! The government policy states that you give me all the information pertaining to my husband. But I am not receiving these reports until a year later. Why?"

* * *

Later, alone in the living room I read through the documents...

"*You lying bastards...!*" I said to myself.

Something was terribly wrong. Now I was beginning to realize I had been lied to for years. I was incensed! I was no longer that trusting Air Force wife who once believed everything she was told about her husband from Casualty. I didn't even recognize myself now, and it didn't matter. What mattered now was that as of just a few months ago, David was known to be alive. That meant he had survived nearly 25 years as a POW. Having accomplished that, he'd likely be alive today.

I continued to read some older '60s and '70s documents I had never read until now.

I discovered that there had been a plan to rescue David in '66 under the Top-Secret code name of "Duck Soup." It was terminated before it could ever get off the ground by a telegram sent from Department of State Sullivan:

"Regret Washington unwilling to risk use of Air America Pilots in T-28 for "Duck Soup" Operations. Alternate proposal for use Lao or Thai Pilots unfeasible. None Repeat None has adequate technical proficiency to land and take off from site 98 in T-28 type aircraft. Moreover, because of communications/language and other problems, intercept attempts by

Thai/Lao pilots would pose unacceptable risks to friendly aircraft in general vicinity." There was no rescue attempt conducted.

There was a White House memo dated April 14, 1971 from H. R. Haldeman to President Nixon regarding a meeting with Senator Robert Dole, Wednesday, April 14, 1971.

"The meeting was held at the Senator's request so that he could report briefly on the activities of the National Committee and on his trips around the country. The conversation centered primarily on the reaction to the Vietnam speech of the President and feeling that we definitely have the people going our way and that it's a matter now of continuing to stay on the offensive...There was some discussion of the prisoner-of-war problem and the Chairman made the point that this is a tinder-box that is about to explode as there is real danger of great numbers of POW wives reversing their support of the President. He suggested, therefore, a fairly major move **for cosmetic purposes** and the President asked that this possibility be explored...Other White House documents and communications which cover the following three-week period detail further consideration and detailed planning of **the 'cosmetic' actions to keep the POW wives 'on the reservation'** as Senator Dole suggested. Those documents make it quite clear that **moves being considered are solely for the purposes of 'cosmetics.'"** (Emphasis added)

I was ready to go to war for David!

But m*y God...I remarried.... David would never understand this!*

I knew what I had to do. I explained to my husband, Dean Boatright, what I had received in the mail today. I told him I wanted to put all my energies into bringing David home and that as David wasn't dead, I was still officially married to him.

Dean was unbelievably gracious in his understanding and very supportive. We had the marriage annulled. My path of battle was now clear.

THE WHITE HOUSE
WASHINGTON

April 14, 1971

MEMORANDUM FOR: THE PRESIDENT'S FILE

FROM: H. R. HALDEMAN H.

RE: Meeting with Senator Dole, Wednesday, April 14, 1971

This meeting was held at the Senator's request so that he could report briefly to the President on the activities of the National Committee and on his trips around the country.

The conversation centered primarily on the reaction to the Vietnam speech and a feeling that we definitely have the people going our way and that it's a matter now of continuing to stay on the offensive.

The Chairman reported that the moods of the audiences in all of his meetings seem to be more optimistic than it has been in the past, but there is an overwhelming sentiment, on all sides, to end the war as soon as we can.

The President gave the Chairman some suggested talking points on how to handle the war question and particularly the question of setting a specific date.

There was also some discussion of the Prisoner of War problem and the Chairman made the point that this is a tender-box that is about to explode as there is real danger of great numbers of POW wives reversing their support of the President. He suggested, therefore, a fairly major move for cosmetic purposes and the President asked that this possibility be explored.

At the conclusion of the meeting, the President, the Chairman and I walked cross West Executive to the West Lobby entrance and the President went on to the residence.

HRDLICKA
770 N. MAYFIELD RD.
CONWAY SPRINGS, KS 67031-8018

H.R. Haldeman's "MEMORANDUM FOR THE PRESIDENT'S FILE", summarizing the details of an April 14, 1971 White House meeting between Senator Dole and President Nixon, may not FAX well.

Relevant portions appear below:

"There was also some discussion of the Prisoner of War problem and the Chairman [Dole] made the point that this is a tender-box [sic] that is about to explode as there is a real danger of great numbers of POW wives reversing their support of the President. He suggested, therefore, a fairly major move for cosmetic purposes and the President asked that this possibility be explored."

Other White House documents and communications which cover the following three-week period detail further consideration and detailed planning of the "cosmetic" actions to keep the POW wives "on the reservation" as Senator Dole suggested. Those documents make it quite clear that moves being considered are solely for the purposes of "cosmetics."

CHAPTER 23

David's Vindicator

1990 - "I now had a Mission. There will be no diversion off my path by the U.S. Government ever again...as I fear not." Carol Hrdlicka

With the knowledge of David's likely existence, I sent a Freedom of Information Act (FOIA) letter requesting all of the data and intelligence the U.S. government used to declare David dead, which they had done in 1973. They wrote back and said there was no evidence given at the hearing. They had declared David dead based on no existing evidence.

A few days later I was channel surfing and stopped on the Joan Rivers show, noting that the guests were Marian Shelton and Ann Holland, both of whom had husbands who were POWs. They were talking about the book, *Kiss the Boys Goodbye.* As soon as I heard the title of the book, I was out the door and on my way to Wichita to buy it.

I was no sooner home again than I became deeply involved in what I was reading. I would read a few pages, then put the book down and go out to work with my horses to blow off steam. I repeated the pattern again and again to get through the book. Some of the same things wives in the book were being told were exactly what I had also been told. One of the things was that if any of the families of POWs were to talk publicly, "you could get your husband killed."

My God, Casualty used the same tactics on every one of us, I thought. *What the hell was going on? Our own people were calculatingly working on POW wives to pacify us into submission, finally to the point of even accepting a bogus declaration of death for POWs left behind.*

Between 1990 and 1992 I started getting involved as an activist by going to Washington and meeting with people. I met with both bureaucrats and members of Congress, questioning people and their agencies about what had or had not been done to bring POWs home after the end of the Vietnam War. Their war, though, was over in 1973. In 1990, mine was just beginning. I was naïve enough to believe these people once, but I wouldn't without proof this time. I was going public with this, and what better way than to join forces with Marian Shelton and the other POW wives behind the writing of the book, *Kiss the Boys Goodbye.*

October 1990

I was shocked to receive the news. The wife of the only American service member still reported on, dead of a self-inflicted gunshot wound at her San Diego home, according to the San Diego County coroner's office. The 57-year old mother of five was a founder of the national movement to account for all servicemen officially listed as POWs or missing in action from the Vietnam era.

Police said she left a brief suicide note to her family and was apparently suffering from depression. Her husband, Air Force Colonel Charles Shelton, was shot down while conducting a secret mission over northern Laos on April 23, 1965, on his 33rd birthday. He was captured several days later. While

Pentagon officials had speculated that Shelton probably died in Laos in the mid-1960s, his was the last remaining name on the Southeast Asia POW list, and his wife continued to receive his monthly active-duty paychecks. But Mrs. Shelton was never appeased by official assurances that efforts were made in earnest to find her husband's whereabouts. She often criticized the U.S. government for abandoning her husband and other missing soldiers.

She was quoted in *Kiss the Boys Goodbye* as saying, "Maybe in the beginning it was just neglect and wanting the war to be over. People didn't want to think we'd left men over there, then they got ashamed of themselves, regretted it and just like any lie, it all got bigger and bigger."

In the 25 years since her husband's disappearance, Mrs. Shelton held out hope that he was alive and established her own network of information sources in Southeast Asia. In 1973, she slipped into Laos in a futile search for her husband. She also became a national spokeswoman for the POW/MIA movement, testifying before Congress and appearing on television and radio programs, most recently as a guest on the Joan Rivers Show. Leaders of veterans' groups who had worked alongside Mrs. Shelton expressed shock and disbelief at the news of her death. "Suicide just doesn't fit in," said Frank Borrello, former California State Commander of the Veterans of Foreign Wars.

CHAPTER 24

POW/MIA Chief Colonel Peck Resigns

February 12, 1991

Hopes that our government might find some prisoners-of-war or men missing-in-action were again dashed when Colonel Milliard A. Peck, Chief of the POW/MIA section of the Defense Intelligence Agency (DIA) resigned February 12, 1991. Colonel Peck left behind a "Resignation Letter" that renewed fears of "a government cover-up" that extends from Operation Desert Storm back through the Vietnam War, Korean War, into the World Wars, fifty and seventy years ago: Because the DIA is subject to review by several agencies between it and the President of the United States, secrecy, and silence hamper efforts to locate and recover troops not returned at war's end.

Purpose: I hereby request to resign my position as the Chief of the Special Office for Prisoners of War and Missing in Action.

1) Background:
    a) Motivation. My initial acceptance of this posting was based upon two primary motives: First, I had heard that the job was highly contentious

and extremely frustrating...this sounded challenging. Secondly, since the end of the Vietnam War I had heard the persistent rumors of American Servicemen having been abandoned in Indochina, and that the Government was conducting a "cover-up" so as not to be embarrassed...I wanted to discover the truth.

b) The Office's Reputation. It was interesting that previous exposure to the POW-MIA Office, while assigned to the DIA, both as a Deputy Director for Intelligence (DDI) and as the Chief of the Asia Division for Current Intelligence (JSI-3) was negative. DIA personnel who worked with me in dealing with the office, always spoke about it in deprecating terms, alluding to the fact that any report which found its way there would quickly disappear into "a black hole."

c) General Attitudes: Surveys of active-duty military personnel indicated that a high percentage (83%) believed that there were still live American prisoners in Vietnam. This idea was further promulgated in a number of legitimate veterans' periodicals and professional journals, as well as the media in general, which held that where there was so much smoke, there must be fire.

d) Cover-up: The dark side of the issue was particularly unsettling because of the persistent rumors of a government conspiracy, alleging that U.S. military personnel had been left behind to the victorious Communist governments in Vietnam, Laos, and Cambodia, and that, for "political reasons," or running the risk of a second Vietnam war, their existence was officially denied by the U.S. Government. Worse yet was the implication that DIA's special office for POWs and MIAs was an integral part of this cover-up effort so as not to embarrass the Government nor the Defense Establishment.

e) The Crusade: As a Vietnam veteran with a certain amount of experience in Indochina, I was interested in the entire POW-MIA question, and willingly volunteered for this job, viewing it as a sort of holy crusade.

f) The Harsh Reality: Heading up the office has not been pleasant. My plan was to be totally honest and forthcoming on the entire issue and aggressively pursue innovative actions and concepts to clear up the live sighting business, thereby refurbishing the image and honor of the DIA. I became painfully aware, however, that I was not really in charge of my own office, but was merely a figurehead or whipping boy for a larger and totally **Machiavellian group of players** outside of DIA. What I witnessed during my tenure as the cardboard cutout "Chief" of the POA-MIA could euphemistically be labeled as disillusioning.

2) Current Impressions, Based on my Experience

a) Highest National Priority. The National leaders continue to address the prisoner of war and missing in action issues as the "highest national priority" is a travesty. From my vantage point, I observed that the principal government players were interested primarily in conducting a "damage limitation exercise" and appeared to knowingly and deliberately generate an endless succession of manufactured crises and "busy work." Progress consisted in frenetic activity, with little substance and no real results.

b) The Mindset to Debunk. The mindset to "debunk" is alive and well. It is held at all levels, and continues to pervade the POW/MIA Office, which is not necessarily the fault of the DIA. Practically all analysis is directed to finding fault with the source. Rarely has there been any effective follow-through on any of the sightings, nor is there a responsive "action arm" to routinely and aggressively pursue leads. The latter was a moot point, anyway, since the Office was continuously buried in an avalanche of "ad hoc" taskings from every quarter, all of which required immediate response. It was impossible to plan ahead or prioritize courses of action. Any real effort to pursue live sighting reports or exercise initiative was diminished by the plethora of "busy work" projects directed by higher authority outside DIA. A number of these grandiose endeavors bordered on the ridiculous - quite significantly – there was never an audit trail. None of these taskings was ever requested formally. There was, and still is, a refusal by any of the players to follow normal intelligence channels in dealing with the POW/MIA office.

c) Duty, Honor, Integrity: It appears that the entire issue is being manipulated by unscrupulous people in the Government or associated with the Government. Some are using the issue for personal or political advantage and others use it as a forum to perform and feel important, or worse. The sad fact, however, is that this issue is being controlled and a cover-up may be in progress. The entire charade does not appear to be an honest effort and may never have been.

d) POW/MIA Officers Abandoned. When I assessed the office for the first time, I was somewhat amazed and greatly disturbed by the fact that I was the only military officer in an organization of more than 40 people. Since combatants of all Services were lost in Vietnam and I would have thought there would at least be a token service representation for a matter of the "Highest National Priority." Since the normal mix of officers from all services is not found in my organization, it would appear that the issue, at least at the working level, has, in fact, been abandoned. Also, the horror stories of the succession of military officers at the 0-5 and 0-6 level who have in some manner "rocked the boat" and quickly come to grief at the hands of the Government policy makers who direct the issue, lead one to the conclusion that we are all quite expendable, so by extrapolation one simply concludes that **these same bureaucrats would "sacrifice" anyone who was troublesome or contentious – including prisoners of war and missing in action**. Not a comforting thought. Any military officer expected to survive in this environment would have to be myopic, an accomplished sycophant, or totally insouciant. (emphasis added)

e) The DIA involvement. DIA's role in the affair is truly unfortunate. The overall Agency had generally practiced a "damage limitation drill" on the issue, as well. The POW/MIA Office had been cloistered for all practical purposes and left to its own fortunes. The POW Office is the lowest office in the Government "effort" to resolve the issue, and oddly for an intelligence organization, has become the "lightning rod" for the entire establishment on the matter. The policy people manipulating the affair have maintained their distance and remained hidden in the shadows, while using the office as a "toxic waste dump" to bury the whole "mess" out of sight and mind in a facility with limited access to public scrutiny. Whatever happens in the issue, DIA takes the blame, while the real players remain invisible. The fact that the POW/MIA office is always the center of an investigation is of no surprise. Many people suspect that something is rotten about the whole thing, but cannot find an audit trail to ascribe blame, so they attack the DIA/POW/MIA "dump" simply because it has been placed in the line of fire as a cheap, expendable decoy.

f) "Suppressio Veri Suggesto Falsi": Many of the puppet masters play a confusing murky role. For instance, the Director of the National League of Families occupies an interesting and questionable position in the whole process. Although assiduously "churning" the account to give a tawdry illusion of progress, she is adamantly opposed to any initiative to actually get to the heart of the problem, and, more importantly, interferes in, or actively sabotages POW/MIA analyses or investigations. She insists on rewriting or editing all significant documents produced by the Office, inserting her own twist, or meaning to what was originally prepared. This is then touted as the DIA position. She apparently has access to top secret, code word message traffic, for which she supposedly is not cleared, and she receives it well ahead of the DIA Intelligence analysts. Her influence in jerking around everyone and everything involved in the issue goes far beyond the "war and the MIA protester gone straight" scenario. She was brought from the outside into the center of the Imbroglio, and then cloaked in a mantle of sanctimony, routinely impeding real progress and insidiously "muddles up" the issue. One wonders who she really is and where she came from...

3) CONCLUSIONS
   a) The Stalled Crusade. Unfortunately, what began on such a high note never succeeded in embarking. In some respects, however, I have managed to satisfy some of my curiosity.
   b) Everyone is expendable. I have seen firsthand how ready and willing the policy people are to sacrifice or "abandon" anyone who might be perceived as a political liability. It is quick and facile and can be easily covered.
   c) High-Level Knavery. I feel strongly that this issue is being manipulated and controlled at a higher level, not with the goal of resolving it, but more to obfuscate the question of live prisoners and give the illusion of progress through hyperactivity.
   d) "Smoke and Mirrors." From what I have witnessed, it appears that any soldier left in Vietnam, even inadvertently, was, in fact, abandoned years ago, and that the farce that is being played is no more than political legerdemain done with "smoke and mirrors," to stall the issue until it dies a natural death.

e) National League of Families: I am convinced that the Director of this Organization is much more than meets the eye and is a principal actor in the grand show. She is in the perfect position to clamor for "progress," while really intentionally impeding the effort. And there are numerous examples of this. Otherwise, it is inconceivable that so many bureaucrats in the "system" would instantaneously do her bidding and humor her every whim.

f) DIA's Dilemma. Although greatly saddened by the role ascribed to the Defense Intelligence Agency, I feel, at least, with what I am dealing with honest men and women who are generally powerless to make the system work. My appeal and attempt to amend this role perhaps never had a chance. We, all, were subject to control. I particularly salute the personnel in the POW/MIA Office for their long suffering, which I regrettably was unable to change. I feel that the Agency and the Office are being used as the "fall guys" or "patsies" to cover the tricks of others.

4) RECOMMENDATIONS:

a) One Final Vietnam Casualty. So ends the war and my last crusade, like it did actually end, I guess. However, as they say in the Legion, "je ne regrette rein..." For all of the above, I respectfully request to be relieved of my duties as Chief of the Special Office for Prisoners of War and Missing in Action.

b) Farewell to Arms. So as to avoid the annoyance of being shipped off to some remote corner, out of sight and out of the way, in my own "bamboo cage" of silence somewhere, I further request

> that the Defense Intelligence Agency, which I have attempted to serve loyally and with honor, assist me in being retired immediately from active military service.

Signed: Millard A. Peck Colonel, Infantry. USA

CHAPTER 25

Trowbridge, a Step Down from Colonel Peck

During the period of time after Colonel Peck resigned from the DIA in 1991, Charles Trowbridge filled in until a replacement could be found. On one occasion, while my son David was visiting, he wanted to know who the U.S. postal worker was who was referenced in a 1990 letter stating that his Dad, Colonel David L. Hrdlicka, had tried to escape. I suggested we call Mr. Trowbridge and put the question to him.

During the conversation, Trowbridge suggested that David come to Washington to see him personally. He indicated he would tell David the name of the postal worker. When David arrived in Mr. Trowbridge's office to get the name of the postal worker, Mr. Trowbridge started to back track, as in an effort to debunk the whole issue. He implied that there might not have been any such postal worker.

I found a document that claimed that the information came from a "federal agent" by the name of Pierre O'Reilly. Later I found out that he was a French businessman living in California at the time, not actually a federal agent. I was never able to find him. I am left wondering why Trowbridge misrepresented this information to us, or worse, didn't know or bother to check out the facts. It just reinforced Peck's claims about his department being bullied by authoritative bureaucrats in his resignation letter.

Trowbridge had been avoiding me for years. I was asked by Dolores Alfond, Alliance of Families, to sit in on a briefing at the Pentagon in her place. I was happy to do that. During the briefing, Mr. Trowbridge got up and made a presentation. I had never seen him in person, so when we took a 10-minute break, I hurried over and cornered Mr. Trowbridge. I introduced myself and addressed the issue that the DPMO (Defense Prisoner of War/Missing Personnel Office) was still putting out false information, to wit, that they were still telling anyone who inquired about David's case that he was dead.

"The DPMO's own reports say Hrdlicka's fate is unknown. Do you agree with that?"

At which point, he started off on some long-winded answer and I stopped him...

"No! Can you agree that David's fate is unknown?"

Again, he started in on a long dissertation of sorts...

"No! Can you agree David's fate is unknown?"

He finally whispered, "Yes."

"Can you say that louder?" ...which he did.

I then said, "I'm going to have your job.

After that, I turned and walked away.

Knowing I did not have that authority, I later found out that Trowbridge had been retired. I would like to think I had a hand in that.

CHAPTER 26

POW/MIA Senate Committee Hearings

May 1991

I began sending Freedom of Information requests regarding what had happened to David, requesting specific reports. On July 2, 1992, I sent another request for reports that I had not ever received. I made a specific request for the "code number" or whatever was carried by David for identification in case of his getting shot down and captured. There was a specific "serial number" carried for Hrdlicka, which was referenced in a government report. **No U.S. government agency has been able to find or tell me what they used for identifying David in case of capture. No government agency is able to tell me what the number on David's "Blood Chit" was. Each blood chit had a number on it so it could be connected to the individual carrying it.** The blood chit has been credited with saving many lives.

To explain how the blood chit works, one needs to examine the root of the word "blood," which means, in Victorian terms, "friendship." A "chit" is a "voucher," thus, "friendship voucher." Aircrew members carried a blood chit on their person while flying missions during the Southeast Asian conflict. The request for assistance, in the event they were shot down, was written in English and various languages common to the area.

ENGLISH

I am a citizen of the United States of America. I do not speak your language. Misfortune forces me to seek your assistance in obtaining food, shelter and protection. Please take me to someone who will provide for my safety and see that I am returned to my people. My government will reward you.

BURMESE

[illegible]

THAI

ข้าพเจ้าเป็นคนสัญชาติอเมริกัน พูดภาษาของท่านไม่ได้
โชคร้ายทำให้ข้าพเจ้าต้องมาขอความช่วยเหลือจากท่านในเรื่อง อาหาร
ที่สามารถจะให้ความปลอดภัยแก่ข้าพเจ้า และหาทางส่งข้าพเจ้ากลับ
ยังบ้านเมืองของข้าพเจ้าด้วย รัฐบาลของข้าพเจ้าจะตอบแทนใน
ความช่วยเหลือของท่าน.

LAOTIAN

ທ່ານ ທີ່ເຄົາລົບ

ຂ້າພະເຈົ້າ ເປັນອາເມຣິກັນ . ຂ້າພະເຈົ້າ ປາກພາສາ
ຂອງທ່ານບໍ່ໄດ້ . ເຄາະຮ້າຍ ໄດ້ບັງຄັບໃຫ້ ຂ້າພະເຈົ້າ ມາຫາ
ຄວາມຊ່ວຍເຫຼືອຈາກທ່ານ ຈະເປັນເຄື່ອງກິນ ຫຼື ໃຫ້ທີ່ເພິ່ງພາອາໄສ

CHINESE

我是美國公民。我不會說中國話。我不幸要求你幫我獲得食物。住所和保護。請你領我到能給我安全和設法送我回美國的人那裡。美國政府必大大酬謝你們

CHINESE (MODERN)

我是美国人民·我不会説中国話·
Wō shì Mĕiguó Rénmín. Wǒ bù huì shūo Zhōngguŏhuà.

我不幸要請你帮助我找到粮食，住所
Wǒ bù xin yào qing nì bāngzhù wǒ zhǎodào liángshi, zhùsǒ

和保护·請你同我到能夠給我安全和
hé bǎuhù. Qǐng nì tóng wǒ dáo nénggòu gěi wǒ ānquán hé

Future casualties were assigned authenticator codes, which could be identified by satellite imagery, as in the "JSSA Analysis of the Walking K" described once on NBC's *Dateline*. The 1988 "Walking K" aerial image was picked up by satellite in the Sam Neua area. It is called a "Walking K" because pilots were trained to use this "K" as a distress signal if captured. In 1992, the DPMO analysts were asked what investigation they had done of this imagery. **Four years after receiving it, they testified at the Senate Select Committee Hearing that they were still analyzing it. The government made no attempt to rescue, or immediately go to the location to investigate this distress signal.**

November 1991

POW/MIA hearings began in Washington D.C. I had planned on watching the committee hearings from home on C-SPAN, but when a Russian general was to testify, they didn't televise it, so I decided that, from then on out, I would be in the hearing room. My oldest son, David Jr., was a pilot with American Airlines, so he had passes I could fly on, and my youngest son, Damian, was a pilot with American Eagle, so I had passes from him as well. I believe I had about nine passes total from each son.

As I sat there listening to the government officials lying under oath, I was shocked. After the testimony of Dr. Roger Shields (Deputy Assistant Secretary of POW/MIA), during a break, I walked up behind him as he was still sitting at the table and leaned into his right ear and whispered, "You have just perjured yourself," and then I immediately walked away without allowing him time to comment. I could hear Roger Shields calling my name. I ignored him. I went behind the podium where I had a meeting with Republican Senator Bob Smith of New Hampshire, the Senate's strongest advocate for the abandoned POWs. After my meeting with Senator Smith I was back in the hearing room, and when Dr. Shields saw me, he immediately came to me saying,

"Mrs. Hrdlicka, I couldn't tell you David was alive..." at which point I reached up and grabbed his tie, jerking on it and stated firmly, "You couldn't tell me David was dead."

Dr. Shields stands 6'3". I am 5'2".

* * *

Bonnie Sitwell lived in Washington, D.C., and knew her way around. She was a legislative assistant to the Vietnam Veterans Coalition, so she checked me out on the Capitol and showed me all the passages from Senate office buildings to the Capitol. Once you were inside the buildings you never had to go outside. There is an underground train from the Senate to the Capitol Building. We could go down to the cafeteria where all the Senators ate and let me tell you, they had an outstanding menu! The taxpayers would be shocked to see all the perks Senators received.

I also had help from family members on how to find documents in the Library of Congress and was alerted to look for handwriting in the margins of documents, as that usually would have additional information. As I was not a trained investigator or ever imagined I would be in this position of having to prove David was alive, when I always thought you had to prove someone dead, there was a learning curve. Of course, that is what the government likes, the families having to play catchup. The government's best friend is stalling for time, hoping with each day that passes a POW will die, and then they can just wash their hands clean and be done with it.

* * *

After watching General Secord from the Central Intelligence Agency testify at the 1992 Senate Select Committee Hearings on POW/MIA (SSC) that rescue attempts had been run for David, he stated that there should be a raft of cables on the rescue attempts. I was never given any of those cables, if they ever existed, though I had sent FOIAs into the CIA asking for any reports on David. I had sent in a FOIA request for rescue attempts named "Duck Soup." Trowbridge, who in 1966 was an analyst on David's reports in 1966, stated that there was no such operation associated with the Vietnam War.

Later, the "Duck Soup" documents were found in the LBJ Presidential Library and David's name was on them. It was a secret operation run by the CIA. I had been told time and time again that I had been given all the documents associated with David's case.

INCOMING TELEGRAM *Department of State*

SECRET

Action 6
OO RUEHCR RUEKDA
DE RUMJFS 064A 15/0615Z
O 150600Z ZEA
FM AMEMBASSY VIENTIANE
Info 55
TO RUEHCR/SECSTATE WASHDC IMMEDIATE 1872
RUEKDA/DOD WASHDC
INFO RUMTBK/AMEMBASSY BANGKOK 1398
RUMJIR/AMEMBASSY SAIGON 923
RUMSMA/COMUSMACV
RUMLHQ/CINCPAC 1459
STATE GRNC
BT
S E C R E T MAY 15

LIMDIS

EMBTEL 1865

CONTRARY PRELIMINARY REPORT (SEE REFTEL) ONLY ONE MEMBER MEO TEAM WITHDRAWN MAY 14 AND REMAINDER WILL STAY ON TO EXPLORE FEASIBILITY CONDUCTING RESCUE ATTEMPT FOR DOWNED RF-101 PILOT WHO BELIEVED BE HELD IN CAVE AT VH 1257 UNDER GUARD OF PLATOON PL SOLDIERS. AFTER APPROXIMATELY TEN DAYS, OR ABOUT MAY 24, CHOPPERS WILL RETURN TO PICK UP TEAM.

PAGE TWO RUMJFS 064A S E C R E T

MEO TEAM MEMBER REPORTED THAT PILOT CAPTURED MAY 1 ON SECOND MORNING AFTER BAILING OUT. CLOUD COVER HAD INTERFERED WITH HIS ATTEMPTS ESTABLISH VISUAL CONTACT WITH SAR AND SIGNAL FLARES COMPROMISED HIS POSITION. HE WAS TAKEN ON FOOT FIRST TO XIENG SU (VH 1953) AND LATER TO NONG KOU (VH 1958). ACCORDING TO MEO, PILOT WAS TO BE INTERVIEWED BY HIGHLY-PLACED PL LEADERS IN NEAR FUTURE.

SEPTEL IN AIRA CHANNEL WILL REQUEST SAR COVER FOR MAY 24 RENDEZVOUS.

GP-3. SULLIVAN

NOTE: ADVANCE COPY TO S/S-O 3:30 AM MAY 15
PASSED WHITE HOUSE 3:45 AM MAY 15

SECRET

SENT
[illegible]CA

D284
O RUEPWW
E RUEHCR 1109/3333EEEEEE   1965 JUN 2 03 28

D284
O RUEPWW
E RUEHCR 1109 02/0520Z
P 020404Z ZEA
FM SECSTATE WASHDC
INFO WHITE HOUSE ATTN MR BUNDY
P 020335Z ZEA ZFF-3
FM AMEMBASSY VIENTIANE
TO RUHKA/CINCPAC IMMEDIATE 1508
INFO RUEHCR/SECSTATE WASHDC IMMEDIATE 1950
RUEHJS/JCS WASHDC IMMEDIATE
RUMSMA/COMUSMACV IMMEDIATE
RUHLKM/CINCPACAF IMMEDIATE
RUHPB/CINCPACFLT IMMEDIATE
RUMSALA/SECOND AIR DIV IMMEDIATE
RUMALB/13TH AIR FORCE IMMEDIATE
STATE GRNC
BT
~~T-O-P S-E-C-R-E-T~~ JUNE 2

DECLASSIFIED
E.O. 12356, Sec. 3.4
NLJ [illegible]
By [illegible] NARA, Date [illegible]

Bundy

~~TOP SECRET~~

LIMITED DISTRIBUTION

LIMDIS

RE CINCPAC 310700Z

SOUVANNA HAS AUTHORIZED US EFFORT INTERCEPT AND DESTROY DRV TRANSPORT AIRCRAFT FLYING MISSIONS IN SAM NEUA REPEAT SAM NEUA AREA. MOST OF THESE MISSIONS HAVE BEEN OBSERVED IN VICINITY HUA MUONG AND CAN BE SEEN BY FRIENDLY GROUND OBSERVERS (INCLUDING AMERICAN) FROM SITE 36 (UH 4113) AND SITE 27 (UH 5312).

IT MUST BE EMPHASIZED THAT RULES OF ENGAGEMENT APPLY AND, THEREFORE, THAT AIRCRAFT MUST BE INVOLVED IN SUPPLY MISSION WHEN TAKEN UNDER ATTACK.

INCOMING TELEGRAM Department of State

002

NNNNVV HJA475JT 375
*****ZZ RUEHCR RUEKDA
DE RUMJFS 15QA 2172352Z
Z O 212352Z ZZA ZZZ
FM AMEMBASSY VIENTIANE
TO RUEHCR/SECSTATE WASHDC FLASH 2051
INFO RUMJIR/AMEMBASSY SAIGON IMMEDIATE 1016
RUMTBK/AMEMBASSY BANGKOK IMMEDIATE 1587
RUMLHQ/CINCPAC IMMEDIATE 1569
RUEKDA/JCS IMMEDIATE
RUMALC/13AF CAB PI IMMEDIATE
RUMSALA/2ND AIR DIV TSN
STATE GRNC
BT
~~SECRET~~ JUNE 21

82 Action

SS Info

18509

1965 JUN 20 PM 11 03

DECLASSIFIED
E.O. 12356, Sec. 3.4
NLJ 91-278
By [illegible], NARA. Date [illegible]

L I M D I S

OUR MIGHTY MEO REPORT FROM ONE OF THEIR OUTPOSTS IN SAM NEUA THAT THEY HAVE SUCCEEDED IN RECAPTURING ONE OF U.S. PILOTS CAP DURING PAST FEW WEEKS BY PATHET LAO AND HAVE WALKED HIM OUT TO FRIENDLY TERRITORY. WE ARE SENDING A CHOPPER TO THEIR COMMA POST TO PICK HIM UP.

IT IS NOT REPEAT NOT YET CLEAR WHETHER THIS IS HRDLCKA OR SHEL BUT WE ASSUME IT IS ONE OR THE OTHER. WE WILL FLY HIM DIRECT T UDORN AND PRESUME OTHER WORD WILL COME THROUGH AIR FORCE CHANN

PAGE TWO RUMJFS 15QA ~~SECRET~~

I WOULD LIKE TO STRESS OVERWHELMING IMPORTANCE THAT THIS RESCU NOT REPEAT NOT BE GIVEN PUBLICITY. I HAVE ALREADY PASSED THIS WORD TO UDORN AND TRUST IT CAN BE PUNCTUATED BY INSTRUCTIONS T ALL ECHELONS, PARTICULARLY PENTAGON PRESS SERVICES. SAME INJUN SHOULD BE PASSED TO NEXT OF KIN.

THIS OFFICER IS ONLY ONE OF THREE FOR WHICH WE CURRENTLY HAVE MEO RESCUE OPERATIONS IN PROGRESS. THOSE OPERATIONS, AS WELL A LIVES OF U.S. OFFICERS AND OUR MEO AND LAO FRIENDS, COULD BE COMPROMISED AND JEOPARDIZED BY PUBLIC HULLABALOO ABOUT THIS RE

WHEN WE HAVE MORE FACTS IN HAND, WE WILL BE IN TOUCH RE BEST METHOD HANDLING THIS MATTER WITH ICRC AND OTHER ENTITIES WHICH NEED TO KNOW ABOUT PILOT'S RECOVERY. PLEASE ADVISE ACTION TAKEN.

GP-3 SULLIVAN
NOTE: ADVANCE COPY TO SS/O, 6/20/65, 11:08 p.m.
PASSED WHITEHOUSE, 6/20/65, 11:20 p.m.
CIA, 6/20/65, 11:35 p.m.

HANDLED. EXDIS PER SSO ~~SECRET~~

REPRODUCTION FROM THIS COPY PROHIBITED UNLESS "UNCLASSIFI

INCOMING TELEGRAM Department of State

NSC

46-42 TOP SECRET S

Action SS

Info

NNNNVV MJA106SPA931JFA439
PP RUEHCR RUEHJS
DE RUMJFS 119A 18/1155Z
P R 181125Z ZEA
FM AMEMBASSY VIENTIANE
TO RUMSALA/2D AIRDIV PRIORITY CITE 181125Z
INFO RUMSALK/DEP CMDR. 1AD THAI UDORN THAI
RUHKA/CINCPAC 1566
RUMSALB/KORAT AB THAI
RUEHCR/SECSTATE WASHDC 2047
RUMTBK/AMEMBASSY BANGKOK 1580
RUEHJS/DOD WASHDC
RUMBAJ/DEPCHJUSMAG THAI 2462
RUMDC/DET CMDR. 1AD THAI BANGKOK
RUHLKM/PACAF
RUMSAMA/COMUSMACV
RUMALB/13AF CC CLARK AB PHIL
STATE GRNC
BT
TOP SECRET JUNE 18.

16838
1965 JUN 18 AM 8 4

DECLASSIFIED
E.O. 12356, Sec. 3.4
NLJ 91-278
By ___, NARA, Date 6-2-92

JOINT EMBASSY/AIRA MESSAGE.

DUCK SOUP.

1. WE HAVE COME TO CONCLUSION THAT OUR AIRLIFT OPERATIONS IN NORTHEAST LAOS CANNOT BE CONFINED ONLY TO MORNING HOURS IF ADEQUATE SUPPLY TO AREA IS TO BE MAINTAINED. IF DUCK SOUP IS T[O] BE RESUMED, IT WOULD THEREFORE HAVE TO BE ON BASIS THAT FRIEND[LY] AIRCRAFT WOULD HAVE UNRESTRICTED ACCESS TO NORTHEAST LAOS FROM [...] AM TO FIVE PM DAILY (LOCAL TIME). IN OTHER WORDS, DUCK SOUP OPERATIONS COULD NOT BE CONDUCTED DURING THIS PERIOD.

2. WE ARE STILL CONCERNED WITH PROBLEM OF POSITIVE IDENTIFICA[TION] OF HOSTILE AIRCRAFT. IS IT POSSIBLE, FOR EXAMPLE, TO DISTINGUI[SH] DRV AIRCRAFT ON PASSENGER RUN FROM AIRCRAFT ON DROP MISSION?

3. IN EVENT SATISFACTORY PROCEDURES CAN BE WORKED OUT FOR RESUMPTION DUCK SOUP UNDER CONDITIONS SET FORTH IN PARA ONE A[BOVE] WE WOULD NEED TO BE NOTIFIED A MINIMUM OF 48 HOURS IN ADVANCE [IN] ORDER ALERT FRIENDLY AIRCRAFT. IT WILL THEREFORE NOT BE FEASI[BLE] TO RESUME DUCK SOUP AS EARLY AS JUNE 21.

4. YOUR MESSAGE 121140Z (NOTAL) INDICATED OPERATIONAL USEFULNE[SS] OF DUCK SOUP UNDER STUDY YOUR HQ. WILL APPRECIATE RECEIVING RESULTS THIS STUDY AS WELL AS COMMENTS ON PARAS ONE AND TWO ABOVE.
GP-3. SULLIVAN
BT

TOP SECRET

During the hearings, the *U.S. News & World Report* published an article on imagery picked up by the DEA showing a pilot's distress signal in the Sam Neua area where David had been shot down. In contradiction to the supposed policy of informing family members of anything that might involve their loved one, they had not informed me of this very significant development. In a break of the hearings, I requested a meeting with Mr. Robert Sheets, Chief, DIA Special Office for POW/MIA Affairs, to explain this to me, how this imagery did not involve David, since it was in the Sam Neua area. I wanted to see the reports they had that showed that David had died. He agreed to meet with me, but when I arrived in Washington for the meeting, he tried to push me off on an assistant. After much wrangling over the phone, with my pointing out that he had agreed to meet me in person, he gave in and the meeting was scheduled.

They led us into a large intimidating room for the meeting. As I was sitting there with my daughter, Denise, and our escort, a large man walked in without introducing himself and just went and sat down at the end of the big table. In a few minutes, Mr. Sheets came in and sat across from my daughter, who was sitting to the right of me. Mr. Sheets was not carrying any file. When I asked for the reports that showed that David had died, he admitted that he had none, nor could he say that the imagery had no relation to David.

In the course of our conversation, Mr. Sheets started telling a story about going fishing with his Dad. Perhaps not understanding his attempt to draw a metaphor into the conversation, I could hear my daughter sniffling, at which point she blurted out,

"At least you had a Dad!"

The look on Mr. Sheets face was priceless. I then said to Mr. Sheets...

"If it were up to your department, you would have the POWs killed."

At this point, Warren Gray from DPMO, the man at the end of the table, who entered the room first, jumped up and said, "I am a Vietnam Vet and I resent that!"

"I don't give a crap if you resent it. You wouldn't do it yourself. You'd have someone do it for you!" I responded.

June 1992

In the middle of the POW/MIA hearings on Capitol Hill came an earth-shattering scoop. Russian President Boris Yeltsin told Stone Phillips of NBC News that some American POWs from the Vietnam War were taken to Russia and may still be alive. Some speculated that the story may have been confused in translation, but NBC News reported that they had even hired a second Russian translator to confirm that the question was asked correctly and understood by Yeltsin. The story spread like wildfire, being printed in major newspapers across the country. The reaction from Washington was swift.

"This does not square with what we thought we knew. It's absolutely new information," said retired Army General John W. Vessey, Jr., special Presidential envoy to Vietnam for POW/MIAs reacting to the news.

Not only did Yeltsin tell NBC News the information, he apparently also shared the information in a meeting with President Bush at the White House a day later.

"President Yeltsin informed me for the first time that Russia may have information about the fate of some of our servicemen from Vietnam," the President stated, "He has told me he will go to the last mile to find whatever it is that exists about our possible American POWs and MIAs."

As the story developed, Russian presidential spokesman Vyacheslav Kostikov told reporters that a start has been made on identifying the graves of U.S. servicemen.

"Hooray, we finally have someone who is owning up to this," I said on hearing the news.

I really thought that with Yeltsin's revelation at the same time as the POW/MIA hearings in Washington that this would be a big year and that the floodgates were about to open up on the POW issue.

David Jr., in an elevator at the Capitol in 1992, was astonished at the courage of the ladies defending their missing husbands.

"Wow! If I ever go down, I hope there will be a group of you who go to bat for me!"

Iran Contra was happening around the same time as the POW/MIA hearings, and the same people kept popping up, General Secord, Lt. Col. Richard Childress. specialists who go around and orchestrate secret wars. During the time of the hearings, David Jr. remarked to Ross Perot,

"Boy, that's coincidental."

"Where the U.S. government is concerned, there are no coincidences." Perot responded.

* * *

During the hearings, a Senator asked the former Secretary of Defense, James Schlesinger,

"In your view, did we leave men behind?"

"I can come to no other conclusion, Senator. In 1973, some were left behind," said Schlesinger.

We thought that the former Defense Secretary's admission would be front-page news the next day. Instead, the POW community was shocked to find that the Schlesinger bombshell was completely blacked out, not covered by the news at all. Our greatest concern was that it was becoming clear that the federal government in 1973 likely knew there were many service members still alive. Very few who had gone down or been captured in Laos had been accounted for. The agreement signed by the United States and Vietnam in January 1973 to end the war provided for the release of all Americans held prisoner and for an accounting of those who had died in captivity. There was no agreement with Laos, but the U.S. fully expected the North Vietnamese to use its power to get the release of American service members who had been captured in Laos. Former Defense Secretary Melvin Laird testified that the Pentagon had information such as letters, eyewitness reports, or radio contact on American airmen who survived downings in Laos. Laird testified that he told President Nixon that. Schlesinger testified that the Nixon Administration's decision to gloss over the issue seemed to have grown from an assumption "that the bargaining position of the United States in dealing with North Vietnam was quite weak."

"We were anxious to get our troops out and we were not going to jeopardize that if it could be avoided," Schlesinger testified. He was asked again if he still believed Americans had been left behind.

"As of now I can come to no other conclusion," he said.

Schlesinger also testified that he believed that at most only a handful of Americans might have survived the last two decades in Vietnam or Laos. He testified that accounts of torture and beatings that were relayed by those POWs who did come home led the Pentagon to believe that Hanoi may have killed some prisoners. International relief organizations like the Red Cross were denied access to American POWs in Vietnam.

Had I began attending Congressional hearings on the POW issue before the 1990s, I would not have been so shocked at the complete news blackout of Schlesinger's bombshell testimony. Former Congressman Bill Hendon and the daughter of an unreturned POW, Elizabeth A. Stewart in their 2008 book, *An Enormous Crime: The Definitive Account of American POWs Abandoned in Southeast Asia* (St. Martin's Griffin), describe a similar blackout of testimony by an even more authoritative person on the subject than Schlesinger. The venue was a hearing before the House POW/MIA Task Force of House Committee on Foreign Affairs on June 25, 1981. Testifying was Air Force Brigadier General Eugene Tighe, the Director of the Defense Intelligence Agency (DIA). In that capacity, he was the absolutely most authoritative person in the government on the POW/MIA question, and he was approaching retirement, so he apparently felt that he had more freedom to be candid than is usually the case with government officials. Hendon, a freshman Congressman from North Carolina, and John LeBoutillier, a freshman Congressman from New York, were members of the committee:

Tighe...stunned those in attendance by testifying in open, public session that he was "absolutely certain" that American POWs were still being held captive in Southeast Asia. He also called for a renewed effort by the Congress and the administration to get the prisoners home ....

"[Hendon] and I were just totally blown away by Tighe's testimony in public session that the men were still alive," LeBoutillier later said, "*We* knew, of course, that they were [alive], but this was the director of defense intelligence testifying to the fact before the U.S. Congress in open session. I'll never forget it — '*absolutely certain.*'" LeBoutillier went on to say that he and Hendon were sure Tighe's statement "would be big news the next day, not just on the Hill, but all across town and, via the media, all across America." (p. 220)

But it wasn't. It wasn't reported at all, which is why I didn't know that it had happened, and with no press-generated public pressure, the Congress took no action based upon Gen. Tighe's effectively secret testimony.

July 2, 1992

On one of my trips to D.C. I went to the Library of Congress to look for documents. I was reminded by other family members to watch for handwriting in the margins. As I was spinning reels, I noticed a document with the words HOT in the margin. I immediately stopped and read the document. I noticed that all the agencies that this was sent to had been omitted, which makes it harder to research. It was stating that there were 23 POWs in Laos! I was shocked! The U.S. government said that there were only two POWs in Laos, David and Shelton, and they had supposedly died in captivity. So, who are these men and why couldn't one of them possibly be David? I realized that the U.S. government had been tracking the POWs and probably knew where David was and had known all along.

John Fellows, another POW family member, told me that he had the aircraft movements that backed up this document. One National Security Agency document dated December 1982 had a header that read: Subject: AN-26 Flight Activity in Laos:

The following information was received (redacted) as possible radar verification of flights to and from Oudomsai and Attapu for 28 November and 7 December 1982. (Redacted) Records show a flight on 28 November believed to be AN-26 from the vicinity of Long Chieng (TG 8022) to Vientiane, landing there at 1208 hours. (Redacted) Unable to monitor flight to and from Oudomsai because of terrain. Also, on 28 November (redacted) recorded a flight again believed to be AN-26 from the north which landed at Attapu circa 1500 hours. Would welcome your comments on this information as it applies to the prisoner of war situation.

I couldn't believe what I was reading, POWs being moved around Laos in 1980. 1980! *Could this have been David?*

HOT!

R 290845Z AUG 84
FM
TO
INFO

SUBJ: THAI HUMINT REPORT OF AMERICAN POW CAMP IN LAOS
ON 28 AUGUST PASSED TO
THE FOLLOWING INFORMATION REPORTED TO
ELEMENT FROM AN UNIDENTIFIED SOURCE. THIS INFORMATION IS PASSED
ON FOR YOUR INFORMATION. HARDCOPY OF THE THAI REPORT AND THE MAP
WILL BE FORWARDED VIA FAST POUCH. ENGLISH TEXT OF THE THAI
REPORT FOLLOWS:

SUBJECT: AMERICAN POW CAMP IN SARAVAN PROVINCE (LAOS))
DATE: 21 AUG 84
TO:
FM:
1. THE RECEIVED AN UNCONFIRMED
REPORT THAT THERE IS A CAMP FOR AMERICAN PRISONERS OF WAR IN THE
AREA OF THE HEUP VALLEY, BAN KADON VILLAGE, NAM HIANG SUB-
DISTRICT, MYANG LAMAM DISTRICT, SARAVAN PROVINCE. A SUMMARY OF
THE IMPORTANT FACTS ARE AS FOLLOWS: (BRIEF MAP IS ATTACHED)
1.1 NUMBER OF PERSONS IN CUSTODY: 23 AMERICAN PRISONERS OF WAR.
1.2 LOCATION: THE CAMP IS IN THE AREA OF THE FOOT OF A MOUNTAIN,
SURROUNDED BY TRENCH WITH WATER FROM THE NAM PHUANG. THE
CAMP IS SURROUNDED BY THREE BARBED-WIRE FENCES. THE INNER-
MOST BARBED-WIRE FENCE IS CONNECTED TO THE TWO SLEEPING
QUARTERS OF THE POW'S. THE SITE IS COMPOSED OF:
1.2.1 TWO POW SLEEPING QUARTERS (INSIDE THE FENCES)
1.2.2 ONE KITCHEN BUILDING (OUTSIDE THE FENCES)
1.2.3 CAMP FOR ETHNIC KHA LAO SOLDIERS (GUARDS) COMPRISING THREE
BUILDINGS.
1.3 GUARD FORCE: THERE ARE ABOUT 30 FULLY ARMED ETHNIC KHA LAO
SOLDIERS AS GUARDS. FROM TIME TO TIME, 10-20 VIETNAMESE
SOLDIERS COME AND INSPECT THE CAMP (ABOUT ONCE A MONTH).
1.4 COMMUNICATIONS: THERE IS A RADIO TRANSCEIVER IN CONTACT WITH
[illegible] STATION IN VIENTIANE. IT HAS AN ANTENNA ABOUT 500
FEET HIGH.
2. THE AFTER CONSIDERATION, IS
OF THE OPINION THAT THIS INFORMATION SHOULD BE PROVIDED TO THE
ANTI-SABOTAGE UNIT AND FOR THEIR KNOWLEDGE ALSO.

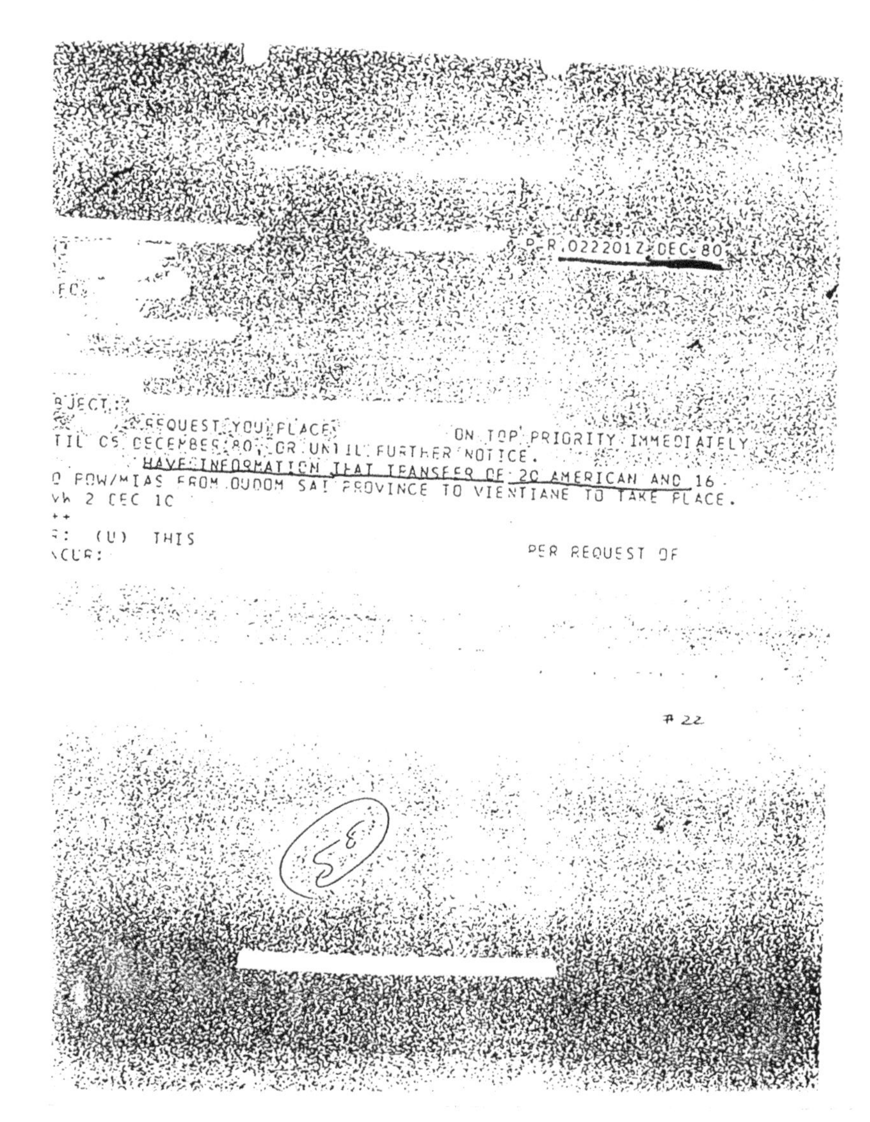

P R 022201Z DEC 80

EC

BJECT:

REQUEST YOU PLACE ON TOP PRIORITY IMMEDIATELY
TIL 05 DECEMBER 80, OR UNTIL FURTHER NOTICE.
HAVE INFORMATION THAT TRANSFER OF 20 AMERICAN AND 16
0 POW/MIAS FROM OUDOM SAI PROVINCE TO VIENTIANE TO TAKE PLACE.
VK 2 DEC 10
++
R: (U) THIS
NCUR: PER REQUEST OF

#22

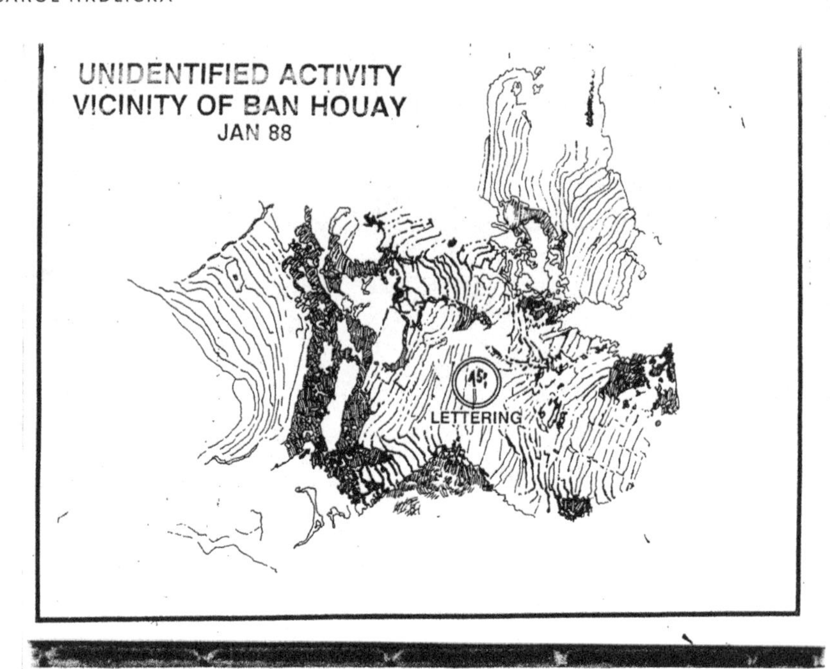

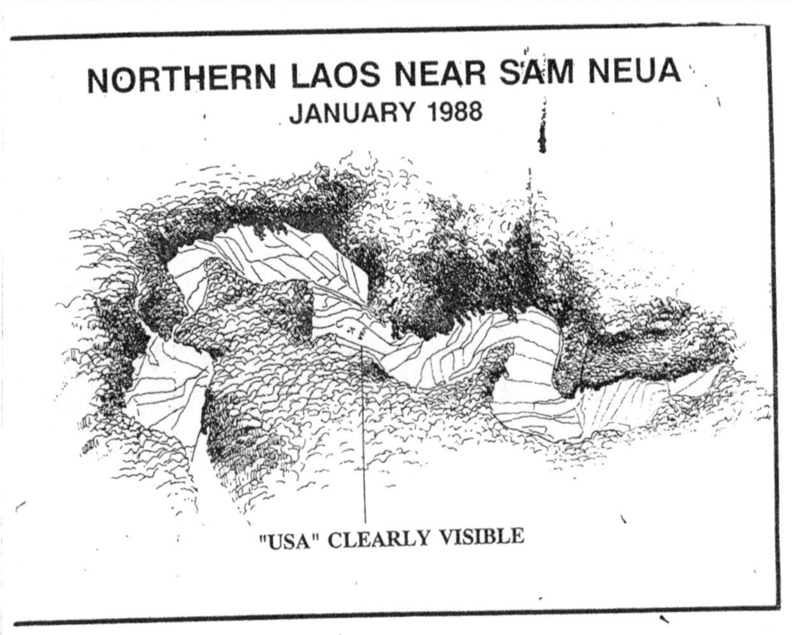

"The following is text of (redacted) message (substantial redaction) because U.S. and Thai POWs have been identified by Thai's (redacted). They will be removed from Attopeu Province. Aircraft will pick up POWs at the airfield on 28 December at 1230 hours. (redacted)."

Still another NSA document dated December of 1980 had the unmistakable subject header: U.S. POW/MIAs in Laos:

(Redacted) On 28 November (redacted) was contacted by (redacted) advised that he had just been informed about a (redacted) which disclosed that 20 'American prisoners' and 16 Laotian prisoners were to be transported from Oudomsai Province Laos to Vientiane before 2 December. 2 December is the fifth anniversary of the founding of the Lao Peoples' Democratic Republic (the Vietnamese backed government currently in power) and Lao insurgent activity against the government and Vietnamese forces in Laos will increase.

CHAPTER 27

My Testimony

October 1992

Senator Bob Smith spent 18 years in Congress, six in the House of Representatives and 12 in the Senate. He said he showed a picture of Hrdlicka to John Kerry before the hearings one day.

"John, this guy is alive (referring to the picture showing David walking). He's perfectly healthy. We don't have an answer. He may have died in captivity. They may have killed him five nights after the picture was taken. But the point is, someone knows what happened to him. Why should we have normalized with these people when they hadn't given us answers on that?"

What drove Smith's passion to fight for answers for the POW/MIA families? Smith's father was killed in a plane crash in 1945 when Smith was three years old. His mother was never told anything about the nature of the plane crash that killed her husband. When Smith went to Congress, he was finally able to get the records from his father's crash and learned exactly how his father died. That motivated him to want to help others find out what had happened to their loved ones. He wrote the legislation to create the Committee for

POW/MIA Investigations. John Kerry was the Chair; Smith was the Vice-Chairman.

Smith said Bob Dole's selection of him as Vice-Chairman created tension between him and Senator John McCain. In Smith's opinion, McCain did not believe there was anything to the live-sighting reports. Smith felt that McCain had made up his mind in advance of the hearings and felt anyone who raised any concern about it were frauds, fakes, stupid, or crazy.

In his efforts to lead the committee, Smith said that McCain tried to block any attempt to follow through on leads involving POWs. There were others who thought McCain was hostile or disrespectful toward those in the POW community during the hearings.

Smith suggested bringing former POW Bobby Garwood in to testify. Garwood didn't come out of Vietnam until 1979. Smith wanted to show that there were others left behind alive who did not come out in 1973. But there was much speculation surrounding the Garwood case. Some had raised accusations that he was a deserter and raised other conjecture over what Garwood did or didn't do while a POW. Senator Smith personally did not believe the desertion claims and had developed a relationship with Garwood. But Smith said that McCain told him that if he brought Bobby Garwood in to testify that he (McCain) would make it difficult for Garwood.

"If you bring Bobby Garwood into the hearing, I'll destroy him," McCain said to Senator Smith.

Senator Smith knew that Garwood was unstable as a result of what he had been through, so Smith didn't want to subject him to that. Smith knew Garwood had gone through a living hell.

To Senator Smith, Senators McCain and Kerry seemed to have the agenda that the impending normalization of relations with Vietnam could be threatened by the hearings and what evidence might be revealed through the testimony. Smith didn't have an opinion as to whether McCain or Kerry had financial interests in the normalization of relations with Vietnam. He did know that laws were violated when Kerry directed that information put together by the staff be destroyed.

Smith stated he was privy to evidence in the Intelligence Community, primarily the Defense Intelligence Agency and research on the live-sighting reports of unaccounted for POWs. The DIA had been taking the live-sighting reports since 1973. The DIA plotted all those reports on a map of Vietnam and Laos. Over 20 years the many live-sighting reports would turn into clusters. If 50 people said they saw POWs over so many years in a certain location, they would take 50 pins and put them on that spot on the map, creating a cluster. If there was one report of a POW in a single location over 20 years, it wouldn't have nearly the weight of a cluster of a dozen or more sightings in a location. Smith claims that Senator Kerry ordered this information destroyed. Smith, as the Vice Chairman of the Committee, felt throttled and "...could not do the kind of investigating that I wanted to do."

Even before the hearings began, Senator Smith received a new piece of intelligence. Between 1985 and 1992, Dino Carlucci, his chief of staff who worked the issue for him, found that every pilot who served in Vietnam had what they called an identifier number. The only people who knew that number was the individual pilot and the Air Force. It had to be committed to memory. If that pilot ended up on the ground, he was supposed to use natural items to spell out his number in a conspicuous place. He could draw it in the sand or dirt, matted-down grass, or use sticks, limbs, or rocks to write that number in any way that could be seen from an aircraft or satellite above. That's what they were trained to do. If the number popped up on a satellite image, the intelligence community would know that pilot had to be in that area. Smith believed the identifier numbers were four digits.

Senator Smith came across some intelligence that showed a number in the corner of a field. The number was discovered well after the POWs came home in 1973. Smith looked at the number and asked himself, "Is this clear? Does this clearly show to me that I can read this number?"

He decided the answer to that question was, "Yes."

The next question:

"Does it look as good as though it had been written on a piece of paper with a pencil?"

The answer was, "No."

But Smith decided it was clear enough to read so that any reasonable person could look and read the digits. Smith ran it by seven people on his Washington, D.C., staff. He did not tell them that the photo he was showing them was even connected to the POW issue. One by one, each member of his staff separately read the four-digit number without hesitation.

The next step, Senator Smith thought, was to determine whether there was a pilot missing with that number and asked: "Was he missing at a time that this imagery was taken over the specific area?

The answer was, "Yes."

The next question for Smith: "Was there any facility nearby where they housed POWs?"

The answer was, "Yes."

Everything was adding up, and Senator Smith felt the next step was to meet with the Defense Intelligence Agency.

When the time came for his meeting at the DIA, Senator Smith met with some analysts who interpreted the same kind of aerial and satellite photographs that Senator Smith had studied for weeks. He showed them the evidence and asked them the same question he'd asked his staff. What did they see written in that field?

"I don't see anything," one DIA analyst replied.

"You don't see a number here?" Senator Smith questioned.

"No, we don't sir, sorry, we don't.

"You are telling me that you don't see a number on this sheet of paper...this imagery? You don't see the digits?" Smith persisted.

"No sir, we do not."

You have got to be kidding me, Smith thought. He shared a look of shock with his chief of staff, Carlucci. The DIA personnel remained straight-faced. Smith and Carlucci left.

Senator Smith then tracked down a man who was a former DIA analyst and now worked freelance as a consultant on similar issues. Smith paid him a consulting fee of a thousand dollars out of his own pocket, not taxpayer money, and then asked him to go back with him to the DIA and look at the imagery and give his opinion.

When they returned to the DIA, the analyst they'd previously met with pulled up the same imagery.

"Tell me what you see," Smith urged the consultant he'd brought with him.

The freelance analyst described the field and other features. He then described the raw materials making up the number, and without hesitation, read the four digits aloud.

"You see the numbers?" Smith pressed.

"Absolutely," the analyst replied.

Smith turned to the DIA analysts who were present.

"This guy used to be your colleague. He sees the numbers. I'm going to give you another opportunity to tell me what you see."

"We don't see anything," they replied.

The analyst brought by Senator Smith stood up and looked at the current DIA analysts.

"What? Are you shitting me? What the fuck is the matter with you?" said the enraged analyst.

They packed up and walked out of the DIA. When they reached the sidewalk, Smith turned to the former analyst.

"What do you think?" Smith asked.

"Senator, I'm telling you they are lying. We have the identifier number, and that number belongs to that pilot. For them to say they don't see it means they're lying. It's clear as a bell."

I had the same reaction sitting in the audience during the POW/MIA Hearings of 1992. As I listened, I thought to myself, *You're lying. You're lying. You're lying.*

As I sat in the SSC hearings listening to the testimony of government witnesses, I was asking myself, *why aren't they looking for the POWs, and as I sat there, it came to me: they aren't looking because they know where they are!*

At one point, I was invited to testify before the committee and debated whether that was something I wanted to do. I had a fear of talking in front of people. I never wanted attention focused on me even when I was in school and would always sink in my seat at the back of the room if the teacher was looking around the room to call on someone. I would be sick to my stomach for days if I knew I was going to have to recite anything in front of the class. But I decided that I had to be David's voice, and I was so angry I knew I could do it.

As I sat in the hotel room by myself the night before my testimony, I reflected, *what in the world was some little peon like me doing testifying before a Senate Committee?* I was horrified, so I kept reading my statement over and over again to memorize it. If I hadn't been so angry about the betrayal of David by the U.S. government, I would never have been able to testify.

The next day in the committee hearing room, they had coffee for us before the hearing started. I was talking to Senator Kerry and I said,

"What is it going to be like to answer some questions?"

Kerry looked down at me and said, "I don't answer questions. I ask them."

I was doing fine until we stood up to take the oath. Then the magnitude of what I was about to do hit me, and I started shaking uncontrollably. I was shaking so badly I dared not reach for the glass of water in front of me. I had taken a cold medication, and my mouth was very dry, but I dared not reach for the water. As I held up the capture photo of David for all to see, I had to rest my arm on the table so it wouldn't shake.

I am Carol Hrdlicka, wife of Colonel David Hrdlicka.

Chairman and committee members. I am here today to make the statement in the name of my husband, Colonel David Hrdlicka, who cannot be here because his government knowingly – and I emphasize ***knowingly*** – abandoned him, as evidenced by the testimony before this committee; they denied David the opportunity of knowing his children and his grandchildren. David was a known POW, and to this day, there is no evidence David has not survived. He was captured by the Pathet Lao on May 18, 1965. His post-capture picture appeared in the *Pravda* newspaper in 1966. This is a man who is definitely in good health. I mean, he didn't get banged up bailing out.

David wrote a letter to the Prince Souphanoupohing of Laos asking for his release. There was a rescue attempt made in 1966 or 1967 which General Secord testified to before this committee. General Secord also testified there were men still alive as late as 1973. A statement reportedly made by David was recorded from a radio broadcast in Laos. In l968, David was interviewed by a Russian reporter, evidence that David had survived as late as 1968.

Senators, this is my evidence that my husband was alive and survived at least three years in the hands of the Laotian Government. There is no evidence that he has not survived to date. In 1977, the Air Force Casualty Office contacted me and advised me that they were going to review David's case, and unless I had any new evidence that he was alive, they were going to declare him dead. I then stated that I had no evidence since I was not allowed access to intelligence.

Why is it that the burden of proof is always on the families? They informed me that they had no new evidence that he had not survived, but they were going to declare him dead anyway. They assured me they would nevertheless continue investigating his case.

As the years went by, I began reading newspaper articles indicating that there may be POWs still alive in Southeast Asia. I received my first live sighting report in 1990, and then my next one in July 1990, at which point I realized that the government had betrayed my trust.

David was a dedicated military person. He was prepared for whatever might happen to him as a product of war, but he would never have believed that his own government would have abandoned him.

David carried a blood chit which I consider to be a contract between David and the U.S. government, and this is a blood chit, and in English on the blood chit it says, 'I am a citizen of the United States of America. I do not speak your language. Misfortune forces me to seek your assistance in obtaining food, shelter, and protection. Please take me to someone who will provide for my safety and see that I am returned to my people. My government will reward you.'

I consider the government as defaulting on their end of the contract. I have asked the Defense Intelligence Agency for their help many times to help answer the questions on these reports, as well as follow-ups, but have received nothing but stonewalling from that agency. I have asked to see the DIA's evidence that David had not survived. They tell me they have no evidence to this date that he is not alive. If there is no evidence these men are dead, then why can't we consider this as evidence that they are alive?

Senator Durenberger from Minnesota has made references to David being seen in and around Moscow. The references were made on two separate occasions, the first in 1988 in a speech before some vets at an American Legion post, and again at which time Senator McCain was present, and again in July 1990 on a local television broadcast.

Senator Durenberger has never given us any further information on the basis of his statements, but I have an addendum to my statement here that goes into length on Durenberger's statement, and I also have his speech here, so when the committee was formed we had hopes the committee would get the questions answered.

I began watching the hearings with great interest in November 1991. I intended to watch from my home, but after the second hearing I realized that the important parts may not be televised. They did not televise the Mooney-Minarcin testimony, which I think was critical. I find it interesting that this testimony was not televised since these men were former members of the NSA and in a position to witness the movements of POWs after capture.

There were many times when the committee seemed truly intent upon getting the answers. Now, almost one year later, this committee will come to the only conclusion possible, that the U.S. government cut the best deal it could with Vietnam and knowingly left American servicemen behind, alive, in Southeast Asia.

If our government would release the information unredacted and the pictures of our servicemen being tortured and executed, I believe this nation would have a consensus that we should deal with them on the issue of normalization as they have dealt with us in warfare – the brutal execution and torture of anyone or anything that stands in their way and negotiate while the pressure is on the opponent.

This nation could learn a great deal about negotiating from these people. They know when time is on their side, and if it's not, they don't negotiate. When time is on their side, they don't budge an inch. If the pressure is not there, time is on their side, and don't be fooled, they know it. If you keep dropping these crumbs, they're going to get the whole cake for nothing and be rewarded for their inhumane practices, and time will kill our men who remain alive in their hands today.

"My concern is that this committee sounds more and more like former committees and government officials in that if it is inconvenient to have POWs, they redefine them as MIAs. If the evidence points to live POWs, they change the definition of evidence.

If a one-time holder of the highest classification and keeper of this nation's most sensitive secrets testifies about live POWs, they will redefine him as unreliable and untrustworthy.

If the number of the missing appears to be too great, they will reduce the number.

If normalization is unpalatable to the American public, they will call it a road map and allow our corporations to do business in the interim.

If satellite imagery indicates men are signaling with specific distress codes known only to these men, then we dismiss it as a natural phenomenon. Now, could we take a reality check here and apply simple logic?

If they have these men, and in many cases we know they did, where are they? If they kept as meticulous records of shoot-downs, subsequent capture and internment, as we know they have throughout history, as we have witnessed firsthand in Senator McCain's case, if they held our men past the end of the war, as they historically have in past conflicts with other powers, where are they?

Senator Kerry, why haven't the radio intercepts mentioned in the August hearings been declassified? Also, Senator Kerry, I do not understand your motivation for opening any trade with Vietnam. When we have opened trade with Laos, they still have not cooperated in getting the answers on the POW issue, so when you talk of easing restrictions on Vietnam, you are encouraging their same lack of cooperation. I would pose one more thought to you, and that is, if it is proven that opening the trade doors was a death warrant for our POWs, could you live with that?

Senator Kerry, you offered to help me get to Laos. I have an additional request. Would you be willing to set up a meeting between the family members and the same Vietnamese officials who you met with on your recent trip?

Senator McCain, as a family member, it is of great concern to me that on every occasion you give the Vietnamese the benefit of the doubt instead of the families. Senator McCain, if you were still in captivity, would you not want your family to continue to press for the answers and for your release.

Senator McCain, I would like to remind you, we are not the enemy. We just feel we have the right to know the truth about the ones we love.

As family members, we have been lied to and misled. Sir, we don't need a devil's advocate. What we need is someone to get these men home.

And why is the burden of the proof on the families that there are live POWs. The question is not whether they are alive today or not, but simply – you had them, what did you do with them?

In closing, I want to express my gratitude to Senator Smith and Senator Grassley for their tireless efforts on behalf of the families of veterans and concerned citizens, but most of all on behalf of the servicemen.

Senator Kerry, you and the other Senators of this panel have asked some hard questions and demanded answers. I thank you for that."

I hope that this committee has the courage and integrity to do what no other administration has to date. I ask the committee to send the following letter to President Bush and the President-Elect, Clinton.

Dear President Bush,

As a long-suffering family member, I want to thank you and applaud you for your support of our investigation during the year. Your efforts have helped create the recent breakthrough in access to wartime artifacts and other materials.

I am concerned, however, that the breakthrough and access has shed light on only a few cases of missing men. If the Vietnamese have flight suits, then they must be able to tell us what happened to the men who wore them. I am anxious that in rewarding Vietnam's new openness we are in danger of losing perspective on just how little Vietnam actually has done so far to account for our POWs and MIAs during the past 20 years.

In addition, I am concerned that all actions required by law have not been undertaken so as to secure the release of U.S. POWs who might still be alive. Section 1732 of Title 22 of the U.S. Code, also known as Act July 27, 1868, 15th Statute 224 provides:

Whenever it is made known to the President that any citizen of the United States has been unjustly deprived of his liberty by or under the authority of any foreign government, it shall be the duty of the President forthwith to demand that government the reason of such imprisonment.

And if it appears wrongful and in violation of the right of American citizenship, the President shall forthwith demand release of such citizen.

> And if the release so demanded is unreasonably delayed or refused, the President shall use such means, not amounting to acts of war, and not otherwise prohibited by law, as he may think necessary and proper to obtain or effectuate the release. And all the facts, proceedings relative thereto shall, as soon as practical, be communicated by the President to Congress.
>
> Therefore, Mr. President, I hereby officially inform you that my husband and other citizens of the United States have been unjustly deprived of their liberty by the governments of Vietnam and Laos. I call upon you to demand the reason for their continued imprisonment, and to demand their immediate release.
>
> In the event that Vietnam and Laos refuse to release our men, I await your report to Congress on the actions that you have taken to effectuate their release. The law does not require proof of specific identities in any legal or secular sense as a condition for your action, but only requirements of U.S. law first must be satisfied that citizens are imprisoned.
>
> Nor is the law satisfied by accounting of the dead. Intelligence files on live sightings, radio intercepts, and photography overwhelmingly support your duty to demand their release before progress or economic or diplomatic relations can advance the requirements of the U.S. law must be satisfied.

* * *

As I read the law at the end of my testimony into the record, Kerry said, "Thank you."

I said, "I'm not finished."

"We need to wrap it up," Kerry responded.

I add, "I also ask the Committee to admit that a mistake was made, that men were left behind alive and require the Vietnamese to account for their whereabouts. It's not a question whether there is evidence of live Americans being held against their will or not. The question is, again. You had them. What did you do with them? Give them back. And I thank you."

"Thank you, Mrs. Hrdlicka," Kerry said, "Thank you for the letter and let me take that under advisement."

Kerry then turns to Mrs. Collins, the next family member to testify and wife of a pilot POW. He later came back to me.

"Now I want to ask you a question, Mrs. Hrdlicka. You say you know your husband is alive. I mean you believe it. Now we are all operating with the presumption that our government should have operated under a long time ago. There is no burden that should be put on you to prove that your husband is dead. And, if somebody is not known to be dead, they should presume they are alive until we find the information that says otherwise.

"But I do not have, and I do not believe this committee has, evidence you have shown us and beyond some of the evidence that we have collected about the potential of somebody being held. We cannot say, I do not think, and I think you would agree with me that we can believe your husband is alive. But I cannot say to you, I do not think, that I know he is alive today. I do not have evidence that says that. It is a presumption. I can work from the presumption, and we should. Do you see what I am saying?"

"The last 'presumption,' as you say, was not a presumption. The last known **fact** was that David was alive," I countered.

"I accept that. I absolutely accept that."

"Okay," I answered.

"And as of that date, he was definitely a prisoner. And your husband was, absolutely, a prisoner. No question in my mind," Kerry confirmed.

"In a court of law, if you don't have a body, you don't have a death, right?" I asked, fully realizing what Kerry was trying to do, insinuating that I was living in the past in denial of the present.

"I agree with you," Kerry stated, "We totally concur, but we cannot say that we know he is alive...we cannot say...."

And I interrupt Kerry – "We know that he is not dead because we do not have a body," I reiterated, "So, when you say we know he is not dead, then what is the alternative? If he is not dead, then he is alive, right?"

"Not necessarily."

"Then, what is he?"

"He is..."

I interrupted Kerry...again....

"If he's not dead, then what is he?"

"He is last known to be alive in 1973. That's what there is. Last known to be alive in 1973."

"That's right. But he's not known to be dead."

"I absolutely agree with you. Therefore, you do not close his case. No, but there's a difference."

Senator Smith was watching my testimony closely. As he watched, he felt compassion. *This poor woman, she's just trying to find out what happened to her husband. She shouldn't have to be fighting our own government to get the truth. It's bad enough to be fighting the North Vietnamese to get the truth.*

Smith knew that there was intelligence to show David was alive, or had been alive, well after his shoot-down. There was no evidence to suggest he was still alive. Those things should have been shared with the family. Smith hated the fact that the government was so hostile to the families who were trying to get answers to the most important questions of their lifetime.

The testimony continued.

* * *

"They didn't close my husband's case, but they declared him dead," I stated to Senator John Kerry.

"I disagree with that," said Kerry, "but you see, we are on the same wavelength."

"I realize that."

"I am just asking you to think along with me and come to the point where I hope you would agree with what I am saying. I'm saying you cannot know that your husband, David, is alive."

"Well, let's put it this way. I know in here (I put my hand over my heart) that David is alive because of my feeling. I've been through this with other family members. And when you are in a situation like this...we have had one of our pilots in our squadron who was shot down nine days before David. We all presumed he was dead, including his wife, because of the report. But you have a certain feeling. I consider myself a realistic person. I know that if David were dead, I would know it. I would feel finality."

"Carol, no one should challenge that. And I do not. So, I respect whatever feeling you have in your heart, and we hope with you. But I need this committee and all of us to try and help make some judgments about what we are interpreting, evidentiary and otherwise. We are not going to try to stomp on what is in your heart. I mean, that is not our objective.

"But let's just say with satellite imagery, which I have not discredited because I do not believe a Laotian farm boy went out and stamped that in the grass. Now we are going to have to prove that."

"We are going to examine that tomorrow," Kerry replied. "I personally believe that it would be very salutary for you and others with that kind of question to go to these places. I really do believe that."

"Oh, I would go. I would like to see..."

"I think our government would help make that happen. I think we ought to facilitate the process. You are not excavators. You are not experts. But I have to tell you, there is an enormous amount of visceral input that can come from going and being there, talking to people, getting a sense of the possibilities. I am all for you. I think it would be very helpful."

"The problem I have is that I truly believe that the only way we can get answers to these men are through the governments of countries like Laos, now we have....they have no incentive to deal with us. They already have what they want."

"I know, but you see, there is a great distinction here between Laos and Vietnam. Admiral, I know some people, I see a head shaking, and everybody says no, they are totally controlled by Vietnam."

"Yes, they are," I agreed.

"I must tell you folks, I have been there. I do not think the ambassador would tell you that. Most of the people in the country would tell you that. There was a period when they were. Indeed, the Pathet Lao were."

"Are you going to tell me that the Vietnamese are not in the northern part of Laos to this day and have a great deal of influence?" I asked.

"I am going to tell you that they do with respect to the northern part of Laos and in certain parts. In fact, the government of Laos does not have great control over its own country, which is a reality we have to take into account when you start to talk about accountability."

* * *

After my testimony and reflecting on the back and forth between Kerry and me, I was totally disappointed in myself and my answers. The response I should have given Kerry's questions about David should have been that there was no EVIDENCE to show David died. I had asked many government agencies for evidence that David had died and was told there was none.

Carol Hrdlicka testifying before 1992 SSC Hearing

CHAPTER 28

Trip to Russia

After the committee hearings ended, Senator Kerry promised there would be more investigation, but that turned out to be false. No further follow-up was done. That turned out to be Senator Kerry's and Senator McCain's motivation for the hearings, to establish that all the POWs were dead. But when Secretary of Defense Schlesinger testified that men had been left behind—as DIA Director Tighe had done earlier—that made it more difficult. Still, they managed to get normalization with Vietnam pushed through over the families' objections.

1992

I first heard of Ivan Shchedrov at the hearings. When I returned home from the hearings, I began going through a file that I had received in 1977 but had never gone through. I found Shchedrov's letter there. I had received the file November 21st, 1977. I believed this was the date that the Feds used to declare all unaccounted-for POWs legally dead to their families. I felt the government was using unrelated reports to "kill them off."

I made many trips to Washington...two, three times a year after the SSC Hearings. During the SSC Hearings, I was there for every session. Orson Swindle, politician, and former POW, told me, "Your husband, David, is still alive." He had reached that conclusion while in a POW camp in Hanoi where they were showing films of other POWs. The only reason he knew it was David was because Swindle's cellmate was Robert Peel, an F-105 Pilot who knew David from Takhli and identified him as "walking around." He said the film was in color, Vietnamese propaganda...not in American possession.

I did find a document that talked about a film.

In a recent interview, Peel denied that there was a film but does recall seeing a picture of Hrdlicka while still in custody at the Hanoi Hilton.

In the first few years after David was shot down, McConnell Air Force Base would call the wives on base with missing loved ones to come and view films of prisoners they had received so that we could identify anyone we might know. The wives then knew that the Vietnamese were photographing POWs.

On one of our many trips to D.C. in the early 1990s, David Jr. and I had a meeting with Senator Bob Dole to get his help in getting David's file declassified and given to me. As David, Jr., started his presentation, he held up a captive picture of his father....and Dole screamed and yelled....

"I'm sick and tired of those fake photos!"

I then responded to him, "How dare you! I have had this picture in my possession since 1966! How dare you say that!"

Dole backtracked. He explained it was at a time when there was a lot of POW activity and conversation and there were photos coming out of Southeast Asia. In my opinion, he was trying to debunk the story that David might still be alive.

My son, David Jr. was present and taking the scene in.

"Now, Mom, don't yell at them. You be nice," my son cautioned me.

David, Jr., would often react, knowing I could get frustrated when seeking answers about his father. But after that meeting, David Jr. never said that to me again. I developed a reputation for being tough and sometimes difficult in Washington.

I received a call from Paul Reiff, who explained that he lived in Seattle, Washington, and had seen me on TV. He informed me that he made frequent trips to Russia. I had been interested in Russia, since, as a former classmate of David's, Senator Durenberger from Minnesota had made a statement on a local radio station that David had been seen in and around Moscow. When I met with the Senator in his office, he later denied that he had made that statement, but I had it on tape, showing him making the statement. I then had several conversations about that with Paul Reiff, and Paul agreed to take my son, David, and me to Russia. The plan was then set in motion. The purpose of the trip was to meet with Asa Shchedrov, who was the wife of Ivan Shchedrov, the Russian correspondent who interviewed David in captivity in 1968.

June 1993

David Jr. and I made the trip to Moscow, and as we are driving to our lodgings I was amazed at how all the white buildings looked grey, no doubt due to the polluted air, and there were cars by the roadside completely stripped with nothing left but the empty frame.

We had an apartment that Paul had sublet for us. We were on the 13th floor, so we had a long elevator ride. As the days progressed, the ride in the small elevator smelled terrible as it was used as a urinal. There was a big elevator that didn't smell quite as bad, so we always tried to take that one to our apartment. My son would laugh at me watching which elevator would arrive first. As we would leave the apartment the smell of garbage would hit you. I told David I would never forget that smell!

Paul had set up a meeting with a general from the KGB. As we were walking into the building, I noticed a terrible storm was brewing. It was growing darker and more threatening by the minute. A track in the floor was pointed out to me, with doors hidden in the wall. David Jr. took that opportunity to make the comment that there were probably many people who never exited the building once they entered.

David Jr. Paul, and I walked down the first-floor hallway. The lights in the building were flickering and dim, as if the electricity weren't functioning properly. We reached an elevator which opened. Paul noticed something strange. Most Russian elevators that they'd had the fortune of riding in were filthy, often full of urine, graffiti, and trash. But this elevator, which was also much larger, was spotless, highly polished stainless steel.

The door closed and the elevator rose. We exited the elevator a few floors later. We walked down the hallway and into what was a major meeting room. The windows of the room faced Dzerzhinsky Square. The Kremlin was directly across the way. The room was large, pre-Stalin, entirely wood paneled with Old Russian carved, highly polished wood. What an impressive and intimidating environment!

We were shown to our seats as if we were seated in front of a tribunal. There was a long, raised podium or bench in front of them, like a courtroom. The bench was long enough to accommodate six KGB generals and their associates. On the wall behind the bench hung a portrait of Lenin. The three of us felt nervous and didn't know what to expect. While we were waiting for the generals to arrive, we were looking out the window at the developing storm. It was about 3:00 in the afternoon. As the storm rolled in, the room grew darker. Outside it turned black as night. A violent thunderstorm began with lightning and thunder. Paul thought it a fitting introduction as the meeting was about to begin with the KGB.

There was a sudden commotion and the Russian generals entered through a back door and took their seats. They began by saying they were aware of who I and my supporters were and knew why we had come. They very politely asked what they could do. "Team Carol," as we became known, mentioned the Shchedrov article. The generals said they were aware of the article. It became apparent that they clearly had been instructed to conduct the meeting at the request of Yeltsin but did not say so directly. Paul felt they did not normally conduct meetings like this unless the word came from higher up to do so. The general in the middle seemed to be the leader of the panel and was more diplomatic in his attitude. As they conversed, it was a very polite exchange.

"We will see what we can do to assist. And we also advise you to check the state archives."

We were given directions. The building wasn't far away, just off Red Square near the Kremlin. The fellow who appeared to be in charge of the others reiterated that they would attempt to assist us by any means possible, and that this would be good for future bilateral relations.

Paul noticed that one of the Ministry of Security generals did not appear happy to be there. He sat there the whole time with his arms folded in front of him. He was a short rotund fellow. Paul sensed that he probably would do anything to voice objection. Paul, addressing the panel in Russian, mentioned an article that described American pilots shot down over Vietnam and Laos being brought to the Soviet Union for interrogation.

"No Americans have ever been brought to the Soviet Union," interjected the short rotund general who Paul had sensed would be a challenge.

Another guy, sitting right across the table from David Jr., we would later nickname "the leg breaker" because he looked like he had once been an enforcer. He had an intimidating presence.

"We have questions about Laos and about my father," said David Jr.

We thanked them profusely for their offer to help in any way they could. The exchange did not last long, maybe 30 minutes. David, Jr., Paul, and I were escorted out, feeling that we had put our best foot forward. We accepted their instructions to check out their archives.

Afterwards, we all felt the fact that we were having the conversation with a panel of KGB officers was remarkable, but it was not fruitful in terms of gaining any information about David.

"That's the guy who would help you out of the room if things didn't go right," remarked Paul afterwards.

"We were asking about U.S. pilots in Russian custody. It gave them the feeling, I think, that we were overstepping our bounds.

Paul sensed that the Russians wanted to feel out us Americans to see how authentic we were and to see or understand whether or not the request had a hidden political agenda.

We went to the archives, but it was locked and closed.

David Jr. and I later met Paul, and he took us to Red Square and other interesting places around Moscow. We then met Asa Shchedrov at a restaurant.

I wasn't prepared for such an emotional meeting. We both were missing our husbands. Hers had died in 1986. She told me how her husband had remarked at how muscular my husband, David, was when Ivan met with him in 1969 at a press conference in Sam Neua, Laos, in which David was present at the dedication of the underground city named "Hotel Friendship." The city was designed to keep the people safe from U.S. bombings. It had just recently been open to the public as a tourist attraction in Laos.

Asa had believed that David had come home. She was surprised to learn otherwise.

"The last I'd heard, David was alive," Asa remarked.

"How would you know this for sure," I asked.

"Because Ivan would visit him when he went over. The last time he saw David, he was healthy and looking forward to coming home. This was as late as 1969," said Asa.

Her remark about her husband meeting David immediately made me think back to what the DPMO said that they believed David died in 1968. I asked her if she had proof of her husband meeting David in 1969. She said she did, and she gave me the article her husband had written. Of course, it was written in Russian, but Paul could translate it for me before I turned it over to the DPMO to make sure they didn't come up with a different translation.

Anything good that might have come from our meeting soon fell apart because of the attempted Communist coup against Yeltsin. Battles were raging in Moscow, with emergency military rule in the city. Paul was there, tanks rolling down the street, White House on fire. Yeltsin survived. But that event set the tone moving forward. After that it was a new mindset. As a result, the communication lines fell apart, Paul felt, because they lost track of some of the Russian officials who had been willing to help us.

Also, we got wind that Asa Shchedrov was terrorized by an American government official. She was visited by someone following our meeting. Any relationship I might have had with Asa had now fallen through.

After leaving Russia and immediately after meeting Asa Shchedrov, I wanted to pin the U.S. government down. They had told me that in the late 80s and into the 90s that David had died in 1968 from malnutrition. In my mind, knowing what I had learned in Russia, I was flying home to the United States, even more confident now that I had been lied to by my own government.

Later, when I turned Shchedrov's article over to the DPMO, they told me that it was very significant, then they went about debunking it. In all the years since David was captured in 1965, there was never a U.S. government attempt to interview Ivan Shchedrov, and they had known about him as a journalist the entire time.

In Ivan Shchedrov's article, it stated "the voice of the pilot was heard throughout the cave." I knew that DPMO would say it was a recording and the pilot was not there. There were three Russian correspondents who had been present at that 1969 dedication ceremony who had seen and heard David. I set about trying to track down another correspondent so I could have witnesses to the fact that a live pilot was present.

Arnold Beizer, an attorney whom I had met through the POW community, was going to Israel. I had found out that one of the Russian correspondents by the name of Ivan Laboda lived in Israel, so I asked Arnie to try to find him. He did, and Laboda confirmed that a live pilot was present at that media event in which David was seen and heard. He wrote a letter to me confirming that fact and I passed it on to DPMO. Now I have two eyewitnesses, yet DPMO finds a third correspondent who can't remember anything, and they go with his story.

I felt growing frustration that I was spending my time proving David was alive when the U.S. government was devoted to establishing David as a dead POW.

CHAPTER 29

Department of Defense Admission

August 1993

Finally, DOD admitted they had reports of Hrdlicka that were **not Hrdlicka.** However, these reports still remained in David's files. Colonel Schlatter stated there were no sightings of pilots in the caves after 1967, yet I have a report dated 1968 stating American pilots were imprisoned in a cave. There is another report dated January 1970 on a prison camp containing about 20 U.S. pilots at Sam Neua. Another report dated 1973 shows seven Caucasians, and two had an audience with Prince Souphanavong. There is an intelligence report on 54 confirmed enemy camps in Laos. If there are no U.S. prisoners in Laos, then what are the camps for? Over 500 men were lost in Laos. Is it reasonable to think that out of 500+ men, only two men survived their incident? A report stated that the only known POWs to be in the area were Hrdlicka and Shelton. Then, who were all the other men referred to in the U.S. government's own documents?

In a 1992 Senate Select Committee Hearing deposition, Admiral Moorer made the statement, "Once they get moved into that POW status, God help them," meaning the U.S. government agencies had a problem with a man listed as POW instead of missing, which is easier to write off.

In 1992, JTFFA (Joint Task Force for Full Accounting) did an excavation of another gravesite. They continued to waste taxpayer's money when they had documents that showed there was a highly classified record kept by the Laotians stating, "Unless the U.S. government abides by Nixon's 17 points, there will be no information on the missing."

Finally, in August 1993 I asked Ross Perot to help me get into the White House so I could meet with President Clinton to advise him of my husband's plight and ask him to negotiate my husband's release from Laos. Mr. Perot put me in touch with David Gergen who worked in the White House. Mr. Gergen then set up a meeting with Sandy Berger, who I believe was assistant to Anthony Lake, National Security Adviser. As we were waiting to hear back, Barry Toll, who served as an intelligence staff sergeant in the Army and became a POW activist, had a stack of documents, and handed me a picture of a pilot's authenticator number and said,

"Fax this picture to the White House."

I did and within minutes I received a call from the White House and the meeting was on.

September 9, 1993

In 1993, while I was working on the White House meeting, I became aware that there was a memo stating that I would be coming to town for the meeting with Anthony Lake, National Security Advisor to Clinton. My question became, "Why are they following me when they should be looking for my husband?" They really seemed to care a lot more about where I was than where he was. I contacted Senator Dole's office and the DOD Inspector's office and asked why DPMO was following me.

The private memo from A.M. (cryptically named) was written November 2, 1993, to Chuck Trowbridge with the subject: Discussion with Activist.

> Karen Miller called at 0840 hours this morning; she stated essentially as follows:
>
> Carol Hrdlicka was in town last week. Miller asked her about the "Joyce Cook interview of Chuck Trowbridge," and whether she believed it or not. Hrdlicka says she called Van Atta about the piece and asked him if it was true. Van Atta said, "Well, let's put it this way; Trowbridge has stated all of the things as reported at one time or another." Hrdlicka did not believe the Cook article, however, sent it to Freeman along with her letter.
>
> Van Atta has published a flyer asking for $3500 to finance his trip to Laos with Hrdlicka. Carol heard about it, became upset that "Van Atta was using David's name to collect funds," and withdrew from the proposed trip.
>
> Carol Hrdlicka will be in town again on Thursday accompanied by Barry Toll. She plans to meet with Tony Lake.
>
> Van Atta is being represented by a marketing group in Pennsylvania; apparently, you can call 1-800-POW-1221 and order POW paraphernalia. The monies go to Van Atta.
>
> Miller stated that if Chuck Trowbridge wanted to diffuse [sic] the situation with Carol Hrdlicka, she would recommend that Chuck either call or meet with Hrdlicka to discuss the matter (I do not know if this recommendation was prompted by anything Hrdlicka said to her or not).

I wrote a response to Karen Miller dated July 25, 1994, regarding the above memo that follows. It is a shame that I had to consider the DIA as an "enemy." But it was obvious that they were using Karen to spy on my activities and report them to DIA.

Karen,

I was very sorry to hear what Joe Jordon had done and you must know I would have never agreed to such tactics nor condoned such actions. You must understand if I were to have been responsible for such appalling actions, they would have taken place months ago.!!! I think you must put the blame for this whole mess where it really belongs, and that is with your "friend" in the D.I.A. who is Mr. Warren Gray!!! You must ask yourself who sent me the memo? I would say you have been betrayed by that person. I think you will remember when you told me, sometime back, that you were dealing with Mr. Gray. I then warned you to be careful as I did not like nor trust Mr. Gray, or anyone connected to the D.I.A.!! You assured me you could handle the situation. You also warned me that I might hear a rumor that you were working for the D.I.A. and not to put stock in rumors. The reason I have just let everything lie since I received the memo is – I prefer to work the POW issue instead of getting involved in side issues. I did, however, contact my Congressman's office to inquire as to why agencies of this government were concerned about my comings and goings.

I was totally shocked when I received that memo – I did not care what you said about Trowbridge or Van Atta but did not expect you to tell of my Nov. 4 meeting with Lake – and to all people, the D.I.A.! The memo was dated two days before the meeting. We had spent months on that meeting and had kept knowledge of it to a minimum. So you must know the devastation I felt when I saw that you had told the D.I.A. two days before the meeting we were going to meet with Lake. I see that as telling the enemy so they can get ready to debunk anything positive that would have come out of the meeting. Now I understand why what we were promised during the meeting was never fulfilled. Immediately after our meeting, the game of stalling was instituted that in turn gave the "enemy" time to debunk everything we had informed Lake to investigate.

I will never forget all your kindness over the last several years and must tell you I looked forward to our visits. I have been truly saddened by this whole situation – as I trusted you because you were a family member and believed we had the same desire – get our men home! I must thank you for putting me up so many times and I will truly miss our friendship. So lay the blame at his feet. You are in the enemy camp, so they have set about to destroy you.

They have been responsible for keeping this issue under wraps for over 20 years and all of their reputations are at stake so no matter what they promise you they will protect themselves at all cost.

I wish you the best and would never attack your character or judge your personal life so always remember that is not my style.

Disappointedly,

Carol Hrdlicka

* * *

A couple of years later in the meeting room on the House side I was chatting with Warren Gray and the memo came up in the conversation.

He stated, "You got us in a lot of trouble over that memo."

My reply was "I'm glad to hear it!"

That was the first time I had had any feedback.

Our first meeting in the White House was scheduled for Sept. 9, 1993 where George Carver, now retired CIA, and I met with David Gergen, Sandy Berger, Rod von Lipsey, and other associates. The meeting was laying the groundwork for what we wanted to address with the President concerning the POW issue. On November 4th, 1994 George Carver, Barry Toll, and I arrived for the second White House meeting. We were escorted into Anthony Lake's office, Clinton's National Security Advisor.

As we entered the room Mr. Lake said, "This is about the Wyre imagery," which showed he was familiar with satellite imagery, however, that was not our mission. We were there to try to get a meeting with President Clinton to ask him to negotiate the release of the POWs and my husband, David. We never got our meeting. The documents were handed to Kent Wiedemann with the promise they would return them after copying. The documents were never returned.

* * *

Every year the government holds meetings on the POW issue where they do briefings. The briefings are always about remains, never about live POW searches. There are two groups: One is the National League of Families, which has turned into an arm of the U.S. government and only looks for remains; the other group is The Alliance of Families, who looks for the truth about what happened to their loved ones, abandoned POWs. At one of the Alliance of Families meetings, Vaughn Taylor, who was escaped-POW Bobby Garwood's attorney, stated that his firm would defend any family member looking for a loved one. I immediately contacted Mr. Taylor. He told me that Mr. Jan Horbaly would be the one for me to talk to. I eventually hired Horbaly and prepared to file a wrongful death suit against the U.S. government. Horbaly advised me that the first step would be to contact the Defense Department hotline and see if they would give me a case number. I sent a letter to the Inspector General's office with my first complaint, and they assigned me a case number which allowed me to continue to send in complaints, which I did, from September 1994 to May 1995. I sent in 24 complaints. Horbaly told me that when they were done with the investigations, we could file a Freedom of Information Act request that we could use in the future. When I sent my FOIA request into the Inspector General, they just sent me back my original mailings with no follow-up as to what actions were taken. After he had worked for me for a couple years, the federal government offered Horbaly a job in which he would not be allowed to have outside clients. After losing Horbaly, I did not pursue the FOIA for the actions taken. That was the end of my effort to hold the government accountable through a lawsuit.

During this time, I was working with the investigator of a group in L.A. that was looking into developing a TV series. The investigator found documents in the National Archives which included a 1981 report that the Vietnamese had offered the United States 57 POWs. The report stated that the Vietnamese were willing to release 57 POWs if the U.S. paid the $4.5 billion that Nixon had promised as part of the secret peace negotiations. The report also stated that the "DIA knows who they are and where they are," referring to the POWs. I was shocked to learn that the U.S. government had taken no action to negotiate for the POWs.

- Wolfowitz
- Armitage
- Iklé

Feb 1981 mtg —

Roosevelt Room (Cab. Room not

15 people

RR (P), (VP) Casey

(SA) Cap

Meese, Baker, Deaver

Both had telegram / Politburo → then China, Canada, to me

NVN claim 57 men; wants $4 B

Following week — another mtg -- also in Roosevelt Room.

Casey goes to (P) — says checked w/ DIA, says we know who & where they are. Baker angry at Casey going directly to (P).

Summary of 1981 [illegible] iscussion as remembered by Source:

Casey came into the Roosevelt Room from the Oval office with President Reagan and Vice President Bush. National Security Advisor Allen joined them, as they stopped for a moment to talk.

They were headed toward another larger meeting, and Chief of Staff Baker and Deaver stood a few feet away, at the doorway, waiting for the group to enter the meeting.

Casey said to the President: "What do you want to do about the message?"

President: "What message?"

Casey: "The message from the Vietnamese, through the Canadians and China."

President: (To Group) "What do you think?"

Casey: "I think its just China running interference at Vietnam."

VP Bush: "I agree."

Casey: "We can't give $4.5 billion to the Vietnamese, it would be paying blackmail."

VP Bush: "Yeah, I agree."

Allen: "If these are live POWs, we should do something about it.

Baker and Deaver come up.

Baker: "Its time for the meeting."

President: "OK....(to Casey) do something about it."

Group departs room for meeting.

May 1994

On May 10th, 1994, a trip to Vietnam was arranged by Attorney Arnold (Arnie) Beizer under the guise of a humanitarian visit from Muhammad Ali. Our group consisted of Ali, his assistant, Howard Bingham, Arnold Beizer, trip organizer Bill

Bell, our interpreter, family member Albro Lundy, and me. Our purpose was to approach the Vietnamese government with a request to find any remaining POWs. At one of our meetings, a Vietnamese senator said that there could be people held outside their control in villages. Unfortunately, that was as close as we got to any answers about the men left behind. We were given a government-sanctioned guide to make sure we did not go off on our own searches. They were very controlling as to where we were allowed to go. While Vietnam was accepting tourists, free travel for us was out of the question. Everything was carefully planned.

In our drive from the airport on the way to Hue, I looked out the window and saw that around some of the houses were stone walls with glass embedded in them. It hit me like a ton of bricks that David could be behind one of those walls. The tears started to come, and I was grateful for my sunglasses. I couldn't wait to get to my room so I could let go.

Arnie called and said that we were all going to dinner, and I told him I was unable to go. Our guide was now in a predicament as he was supposed to keep us together. After assuring Arnie I was unable to go, they finally went ahead. I stayed in my room unable to stop crying.

During our stay at Hue, they took us out on the river in a dragon boat for dinner. On the boat, candles were passed out and they put them in paper cups behind the boat as a memorial to the POWs left behind who had been fighting in Hue.

During dinner Arnie was drinking a cup of lemonade and a moth flew into it. Arnie put his hand over the top of the cup, entrapping the moth.

"He spoiled my drink. I'm not letting him go," Beizer said.

"You must set the butterfly free," said Mr. Thuy, a Buddhist who believed that all living creatures have souls.

Beizer was incredulous that our guide would have so much compassion for a moth, while his government refused to co-operate to free our POWs, or at least to find their remains.

We were then taken to Danang where we met with American Search Teams, a Vietnamese operation. They gave us a presentation on what a good job they were doing. What they were doing was simply excavating graves, not looking for POWs. Albro asked the major who was doing the briefing what action would be taken if he received information that an American was spotted on a street corner. The major proudly announced he would send a report to Hanoi and would receive word back in a couple of weeks. So Albro made his statement back to the major who in retrospect realized how bad that sounded. Instead of immediately going to the location of the spotting, he would write a report and wait two weeks for a reply. So much for looking for live Americans standing on a street corner...or anywhere else.

We then took a plane from Danang to Hanoi. Ali met with a sports committee and we went to a gym where all the boxers were young kids. He got in the ring and sparred with every single kid there. Kids loved Ali. There were throngs of people wherever we went. They all knew who he was and wanted to be in pictures with him.

We were taken on a guided tour around Hanoi to a museum where they had pieces of wrecked American planes, pilots' helmets, ID cards, and other artifacts of the war. Next we were taken to Ho Chi Minh's tomb.

As we walked up the sidewalk, Bill Bell, our interpreter, said to me, "Look at those big air vents." During the SSC Hearings, information suggested that there was an underground prison system that held American POWs under the tomb. The Vietnamese denied it. I was melancholy the entire trip because I felt that I was actually close to where David was, but I wasn't able to seal the deal.

David was shot down in 1965, but his ghost had been with me from 1979 to 1992. I knew this. I felt it. Between 1979 and 1992, there were reports that there were men seen in Vietnam working on a road who hollered out to passing tourists, "We are Americans. Tell the world about us."

I knew that couldn't be David since he was last seen in Laos.

I was contacted by a Holland group doing a documentary, and as we filmed, I asked,

"Do you believe Americans were left behind in Vietnam?"

"Yes, we do," was the answer.

CHAPTER 30

National Security Council Testimony

1994

The Defense Department put out a POW/MIA fact book that referenced reports indicating that David had died. After I challenged that and asked for the reports, rather than correcting it in the book, the Defense Department just quit publishing the book. The people in the U.S. government will never admit to their mistakes with our POWs/MIAs, and definitely never in writing. I realized this, and I hate them for it. They kill off our POWs/MIAs to save their own face. How long has this gone on over the years and how much longer will it go on into the future before it is finally stopped?

September 1994

I requested that the U.S. Air Force hold a hearing to reinstate David as a POW. I had come into possession of many documents showing that David had survived that I did not possess when the initial presumptive-finding-of-death hearing was held in 1977. But it shouldn't have been up to me to gather intelligence. The Air Force denied my request for a hearing or to change the status even though I had new information and intelligence reports as evidence.

I found numerous reports showing live POWs all over Laos after Homecoming 1973. Nevertheless, the U.S. government still denied that men were there.

1995

A couple of years after my meeting with President Clinton's national security adviser, Anthony Lake, I was invited to testify before the Subcommittee of the National Security Council chaired by Congressman Dornan. As I sat at the table, I pointed out to the committee that to my left sat maybe 20 people in military uniform who were all against my finding the facts on David's case, and all I had was a stack of documents. As I sat watching the different people testify, Winston Lord, Assistant Secretary of State, kept mentioning the men as numbers and quibbling over lists, which infuriated me. David was a living person who had a family. He was not just a number. I realized that they do this as a way to dehumanize the men. After Lord's testimony, I approached him in the middle of the hearing room. At the time, ABC was following me around with the camera rolling. I began to inform Lord that David was a flesh and blood person, and he was on a list of LAST KNOWN ALIVE. I suggested to Mr. Lord that if he couldn't find that list, I would provide him one. I could see in the background a lot of scurrying around and all those men in uniform just standing a distance away. Pretty soon a young lady staff member came to the rescue, approached us, and told Mr. Lord he had another meeting. That ended our conversation.

As I sat in Congressman Dornan's office one afternoon, Al Santoli, a subcommittee staff member, handed me a report to read. The report stated that a letter had been passed by a Laotian to an American official from Major Gould, missing in Laos, stating that he had a Laotian wife and children, and he wanted to come home to the U.S. It filled me with some hope that David had been allowed to also have a life rather than being a prisoner all those years. How sad it was that a former POW was asking to be returned to his country and his plea was ignored by our government.

In between these hearings, I returned home to my normal life and was very glad to return to my horses. I considered Washington to be a phony backstabbing place. In returning to normal life, I felt like I had just stepped out of a sewer into the fresh unpolluted air of Kansas.

Below is my statement of testimony to the Subcommittee of the National Security Council Hearing Chaired by Congressman Robert K. Dornan, dated June 28th, 1995

STATEMENT OF CAROL HRDLICKA, WIFE OF COL. DAVID L. HRDLICKA KNOWN TO BE ALIVE & IN CAPTIVITY. COL. HRDLICKA WAS NEVER RETURNED

Thank you, Mr. Chairman, for having the moral courage and integrity to address the problems of getting at the truth about our honorable men who were abandoned by their government. I wish to express my appreciation to the chairman and committee members for allowing me the opportunity to, one more time, address the problems the families have had getting the truth about our loved ones.

David L. Hrdlicka was 33 years old and a career Air Force pilot who loved his flying and believed in protecting his country. Our children were young, David M, 7 years old, Denise, 4 years old, and Damian, 3 years old. David was looking forward to their growing up so they could share his love of the outdoors. He believed by protecting his country, he was protecting his children and their future. He trusted his government. He would have never believed he would have been sent into a situation where his country would not come rescue him or be denied by the very government he thought he was protecting.

David and I were married when I was just nineteen, so I matured as an Air Force wife. On May 18th, 1965 I was only 27 when the McConnell AFB Commander, Col. Dannacher told me the news that David has been shot down. David was my whole life, and I didn't expect to have the sole responsibility of raising three small children on my own. I always thought I would have David to help share ideas on how the children should be raised.

I was advised that David had been lost in Laos which was considered to be a secret war, and I should not say anything because I could cause David to be killed as a POW by his captors.

It was not until the 1990s that I discovered other families of POW/MIAs had been told the same thing. I always did what was asked of me by Casualty because I trusted them to handle David's case. You see, I believed Casualty had the background and training in such matters, where I was just a military wife without the expertise to do any inquiries about my husband on my own. I didn't realize I could take matters into my own hands. **I believed they knew what they were doing based on evidence when they had a Presumptive Finding of Death Hearing in November 1977 and declared David "KIA." Only recently did I find out that it was an informal hearing, and no evidence was presented at that time.**

But at the time, I followed what I assumed was their authoritative direction. I made an effort to move on with my own and the children's life. It wasn't until 13 years later, in 1990, I received a letter from DIA stating a source had information that David had tried to escape in 1989. That shocked me into reality and into action. Shortly after, DIA went on to "debunk" the source on which this information was based. In July of 1990, I received another report stating a "General Chaeng was suspected of holding D. Hrdlicka and friends." **To my shock and horror, I began to realize I had been betrayed by the very government I had trusted for 25 years. I believe the only reason I received the Chaeng report was because Col. Millard Peck was in charge of the DIA POW/MIA office at that time. Col. Peck later resigned because of the way the families of POW/MIAs were denied the truth about their loved ones.**

At that point, I decided to start my own investigations. The more I questioned and asked for answers from the DIA, the more I was ignored. I asked for evidence of David's dying in captivity and was told they had none. The DIA had used old reports, which they later admitted did not correlate to David, to falsify their fact that he died. The JTFFA were told by the Laotians that David's grave had been blown up by the B-52 raids. Later, the Laotians told them there was another grave site which was excavated. It contained no bone fragments or artifacts. Why do the Laotians keep changing their story? Because that is exactly what the U.S. government has been doing for years. I will give you a couple of examples in my own case of being deceived and lied to by the DIA.

In 1992, I sent a Freedom of Information request in on my husband, David L. Hrdlicka, asking for rescue attempts, all information on an operation called "Duck Soup," Mr. Trowbridge of DIA, who coincidentally did the analysis on David's 1966 reports responded,

"There was no such operation as 'Duck Soup,' and there has never been any rescue attempts for David."

Lo and behold, General Secord testified before the Senate Select Committee that there were rescue attempts for David made as late as 1967 and there was a raft of cables in the CIA on that operation. Just in the last few months, I have received documents describing such an operation as "Duck Soup," which took place in the Sam Neua area in June of 1965.

Mr. Chairman, I would like these documents entered into the record. Guess whose name is in one of the cables regarding the San Neua area? **David's**.

The DIA continues to state that I have been given all the information, when my basic requests are, to this date, not answered. One outstanding example: I have requested the answer to a question being asked in a Stony Beach report where a U.S. Investigator in June 1989 is questioning a General Chaeng "suspected of holding D. Hrdlicka and friends." I have asked for the "outcome of that conversation" for 5 years, and to date I have not received an answer.

I have asked for David's authenticator code, or whatever they used to identify him in case of his being shot down. I have not received that. In 1994, I received documents found by a private researcher, Mr. Roger Hall. These documents relate to David by name, and I had not been provided these documents by the very agencies that tell me they have given me "all the information."

The Chairman, Senator John Kerry, promised, during my testimony before the Senate Select Committee, that he would get the answers on these same reports for me. I have not heard a word from Senator John Kerry. Senator John Kerry promised, on the record, to arrange a meeting for me with the same Vietnamese officials he had met with. Kerry has never fulfilled that promise.

I have offered many times, at my own expense, to meet with any officials and go over documents they say show David died in captivity. Yet, when I have asked for evidence, I am told there is no evidence. The DOD publishes a POW/MIA Fact Book wherein it states there are intelligence reports that indicate David died in captivity. I have asked to see these reports they refer to and am told I already have the reports. Mr. Chairman, I do not have any report that has David's name on it stating he died in captivity. How is it that government agencies are able to circulate false information? Col. Schlatter of DIA has finally admitted there were reports correlated to David that, do not correlate to David (many of which state **a POW died on dates when David was still known to be alive)**. Where is **Congressional oversight?**

Congressman Dornan, I beg you, get the Government Accounting Office to do an investigation of the DPMO, DIA, and the JTFFA to include the shredding of documents in Bangkok. We have reports that show the JTFFA wasting taxpayers' money and doing an unprofessional job closing out cases. They have committed fraud, waste, abuse. The taxpayers' money has been wasted under the guise of investigating the cases of POW/MIAs.

There are documents that show the DIA has known for years that remains of American servicemen are warehoused in Vietnam – why are we still putting young people at great risk and wasting 100 million dollars each year of taxpayers' money digging at remote crash sites? Robert McNamara has just recently admitted he knowingly sent young men off to their deaths (to be murdered). Today we are sending young people into harm's way again by digging at remote crash sites. Don't these officials ever learn from their mistakes? It is high time that the DIA be held accountable for the waste and irresponsible handling of the POW issue through oversight. The DIA has been condemned by their own officials. In a 1985 memo from Thomas A. Brooks, Assistant Deputy Director for Collection Management to B. General Shuffelt, they are charged with shoddy work, not using basic analytical tools, not following up on cases, and all in all, unprofessional. They were also condemned by General Tighe and again in 1991 by the resignation of Col. Peck. It is the responsibility of Congress to make sure taxpayers' money is not wasted. At this point, it would be more cost effective to remove DIA from their current role and go to the private sector where honest, skilled investigators could be hired.

I have exhausted every avenue, at my own expense, to find the truth about David's fate without the aid or assistance from the very agencies that were charged with solving his case. We even tried to take the evidence to the White House in November 1993. The President has not afforded the families the opportunity to present the evidence to him in person. The public is told there is much progress on the MIA issue but, what the public is not told is, there were over 300 men left alive in captivity - what happened to them? These men were never missing, they were prisoners. However, there has been a systematic campaign to convince the American public that all the servicemen are MIA. That, in fact, is not the case.

One prominent problem is getting the government agencies and officials to address the fact **there were men captured alive, held in captivity, and never returned - what happened to them?** These men were **never** in a missing status. Why is it then, the U.S. government officials, such as Assistant State Secretary Winston Lord, Deputy Assistant Secretary of Defense James Wold, and Deputy Secretary for Veterans Affairs Hershel Gober will not address that question to the Vietnamese or Laotians? Instead, these officials consider the number one criterion **remains of these men** and relay that to the Vietnamese and Laotians. On the recent high-level Presidential delegation, the number one talking point was still **remains**. The number one talking point should be, **what happened to over 300 men who were alive and in the prison system?** Did they just disappear into thin air? If these men died in captivity, then the Vietnamese and Laotians know where their remains are buried and should have returned them years ago. The Vietnamese were meticulous record keepers. Did they just lose these men in their prison system? It is a known fact that the Laotians admitted they held prisoners and would not release them until the U.S. officials came to Vientiane to make arrangements for the release of the prisoners they held. The Laotians said they would not release their prisoners through Hanoi. That meeting never took place and no prisoners were released from Laos.

David was sent in harm's way by the U.S. Government into a covert, unconstitutional war in Laos. Where was **oversight** by Congress? David was an ordinary serviceman, so why was he used in a covert, unconstitutional war in Laos when there was no leverage to get him released. David's constitutional rights have been violated, and I need the help of Congress to protect David's rights.

For many years I believed in and trusted every government official. I accepted as fact everything they told me about David's case. However, after seeing the evidence, I realize my trust has been betrayed. What is even worse, the U.S. government has betrayed their honorable servicemen. How is it that for more than 20 years this continual pattern of lying and deceiving the families has been allowed to continue? We have had many hearings and heard many promises, then in the end we are always patted on the head, and business as usual returns. People within the agencies, such as Mr. Trowbridge, are promoted and continued on in their jobs. **Where is Congressional oversight?** I've heard the lies and the promises, yet today, I am no closer to finding the truth about David's whereabouts or fate.

Please, Congressman Dornan, ask GAO to do an investigation while you continue your formal hearings and oversight. Will you do this for David and all the other honorable men who may still be waiting to come home?

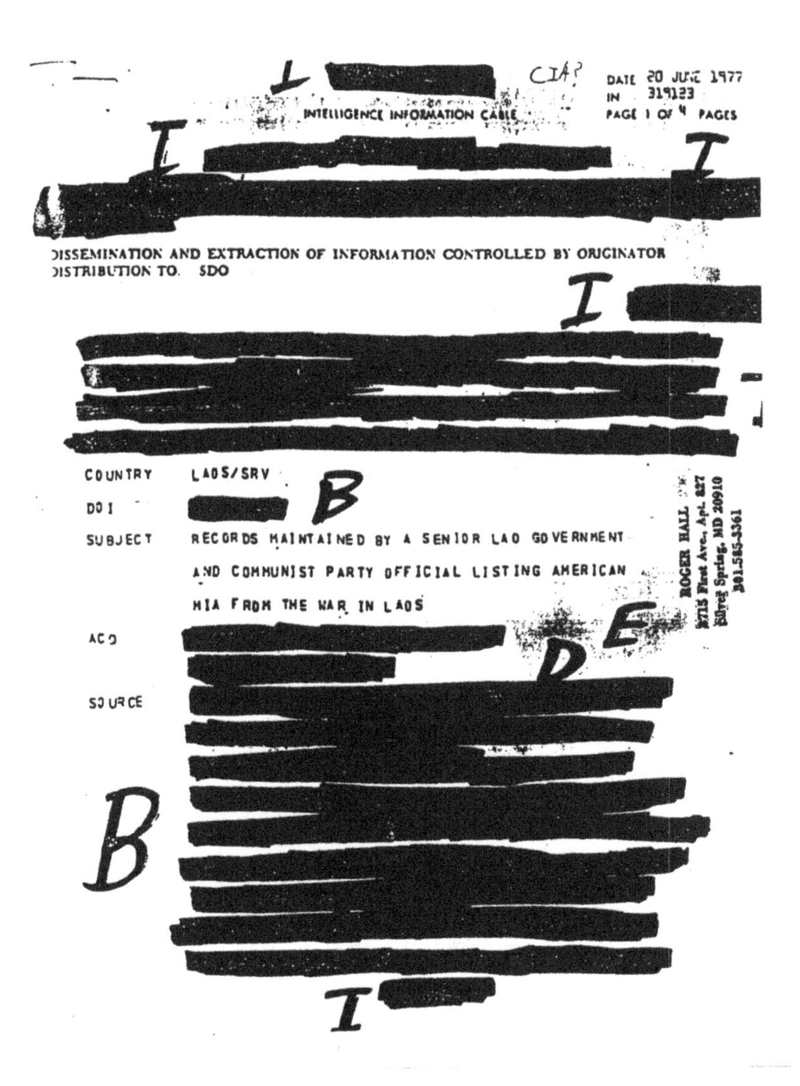

CIA?

INTELLIGENCE INFORMATION CABLE

DATE 20 JUNE 1977
IN 319123
PAGE 1 OF 4 PAGES

DISSEMINATION AND EXTRACTION OF INFORMATION CONTROLLED BY ORIGINATOR
DISTRIBUTION TO. SDO

COUNTRY LAOS/SRV

DOI

SUBJECT RECORDS MAINTAINED BY A SENIOR LAO GOVERNMENT AND COMMUNIST PARTY OFFICIAL LISTING AMERICAN MIA FROM THE WAR IN LAOS

ACQ

SOURCE

ROGER HALL
8715 First Ave., Apt. 827
Silver Spring, MD 20910
301-585-3361

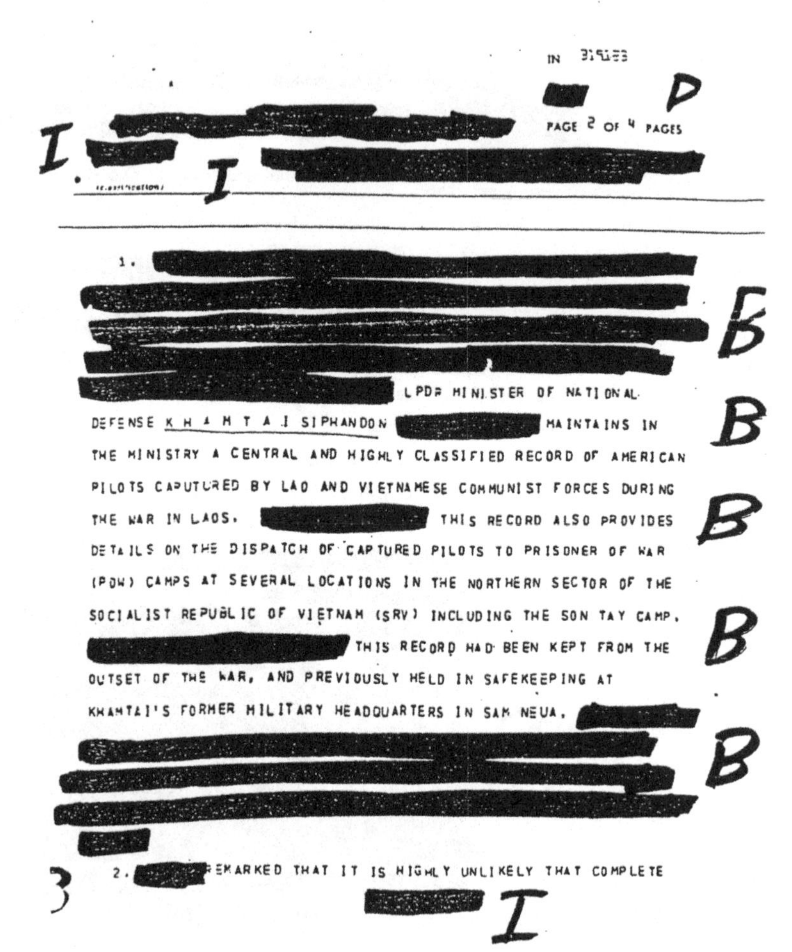
IN 315153

PAGE 2 OF 4 PAGES

1. LPDR MINISTER OF NATIONAL DEFENSE KHAMTAI SIPHANDON MAINTAINS IN THE MINISTRY A CENTRAL AND HIGHLY CLASSIFIED RECORD OF AMERICAN PILOTS CAPUTURED BY LAO AND VIETNAMESE COMMUNIST FORCES DURING THE WAR IN LAOS. THIS RECORD ALSO PROVIDES DETAILS ON THE DISPATCH OF CAPTURED PILOTS TO PRISONER OF WAR (POW) CAMPS AT SEVERAL LOCATIONS IN THE NORTHERN SECTOR OF THE SOCIALIST REPUBLIC OF VIETNAM (SRV) INCLUDING THE SON TAY CAMP. THIS RECORD HAD BEEN KEPT FROM THE OUTSET OF THE WAR, AND PREVIOUSLY HELD IN SAFEKEEPING AT KHAMTAI'S FORMER MILITARY HEADQUARTERS IN SAM NEUA.

2. REMARKED THAT IT IS HIGHLY UNLIKELY THAT COMPLETE

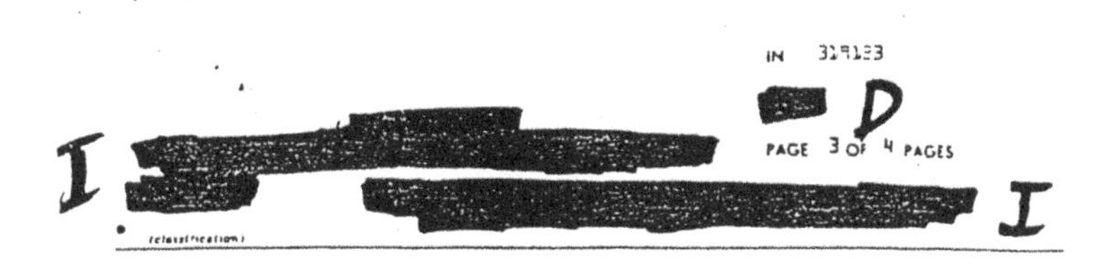
IN 319123

PAGE 3 OF 4 PAGES

(classification)

INFORMATION ON AMERICANS MISSING OR KILLED IN ACTION WILL EVER BE RELEASED SO LONG AS THE U.S. GOVERNMENT REFUSES TO ABIDE BY THE PROVISIONS OF THE PARIS AGREEMENT TO HEAL THE WOUNDS OF WAR, AND THE 17 POINTS INCLUDED IN FORMER PRESIDENT RICHARD M. NIXON'S LETTER TO SRV PRESIDENT TON DUC THANG.

3.

4. FIELD DISSEM: NONE.

CHAPTER 31

Second Russian Journalist to Last See David Alive

March 1996

After filing a Freedom of Information Request, I was told in a March 14, 1996, letter that DPMO had no records of Military Assistance Command, Vietnam-Special Operations Group (MACVSOG) Daily Summaries. Yet another family member received a letter from DPMO stating the MACVSOG Daily Summaries were being reviewed for declassification. This is an example of how families were misled, and the Freedom of Information Law was ignored by government agencies. MACVSOG was later renamed Studies and Observations Group. MACVSOG provided intelligence information to the Pentagon, rescued downed pilots, and destroyed large amounts of enemy material. The U.S. government denied for years the existence of MACVSOG. There should have been information on POWs in the daily summaries. John L. Plaster, a former Special Forces sniper and SOG member, has a book, *SOG:The Secret Wars of America's Commandos in Vietnam* (Simon & Schuster, New York, 1997), that goes into great detail about these matters. Plaster dedicates the book to "...all of SOG's secret warriors, and especially to the SOG men captured but never released."

May 13, 1996

I received a letter from DPMO including a report showing the deaths of two POWs that they correlated to David. For years I had asked to see reports that correlated to David's death. David was identified alive after this report in Ban Na Kay, Houa Phan Province in the same area as Sam Neua. Tham Sua Cave is also in Sam Neua area. A report dated 1969 stated that the only U.S. POWs known to have been held in the Sam Neua area prior to homecoming are Hrdlicka and Shelton. The DPMO finally admitted that these reports did not correlate to Hrdlicka.

Jerusalem, Israel May 1996

Arnie Beizer, the attorney who traveled to Vietnam with me, received a tip about another Russian journalist who had met David. He and Radar O'Reilly flew into Tel Aviv specifically to meet with Ivan Loboda. After arriving, they traveled by car from Tel Aviv to Jerusalem, where they were greeted by a stocky 80-year-old man wearing a burgundy dress shirt with white vertical pinstripes. Ivan Loboda and his daughter welcomed them into their home. It was a warm, sunny day, and they spent much of their time on the balcony at the back of the home enjoying the views of Jerusalem. From the Loboda balcony, they could see stone terraced walls and a stone apartment building in the distance behind them.

But Beizer was there for more than the view. He wanted to ask specific questions. Talking on the phone wasn't going to be good enough. He wanted to get the facts from the Russian journalist face-to-face. Loboda related that in 1969 he, and other journalists, including fellow Russian journalist Ivan Shchedrov, attended a press conference, and that one of the pilots was David Hrdlicka. Loboda told Beizer that he didn't know who the other pilot was. The description of David was what Beizer expected to hear. There were no "aha!" moments. But Beizer now had what he needed – proof from a credible source that David Hrdlicka was alive a year after the U.S. government had declared him dead. Before they parted, Loboda gave a letter to Beizer to be delivered to me.

> Dear Carol,
>
> First of all, let me express my admiration of your devotion to your mission, the love mission. I received your letter, all the materials, met your lawyer, and had a talk with him. Unfortunately, it's not much. I hope your lawyer will tell you about my general considerations of the matter. As to fact, I can definitely confirm the press conference took place in 1969. It was the only press conference in the region with the participation of American pilots I have ever attended. I write "pilots" though I do not remember exactly how many were there, but it seems to me there were two. I know exactly that the pilots talked, but I, myself, did not talk with them.
>
> I wish you every success and hope that your efforts will end in bringing your husband home in the nearest future, the more so that the political situation in the region of interest develops favorably. I also hope you will inform me how things go.
>
> Best regards,
>
> Ivan Loboda

June 23, 1996

This letter from the POW/MIA Office is self-explanatory:

Dear Mrs. Hrdlicka,

I wanted to confirm some important information which our Air Force Casualty and Family Support Officer, Major David Moore, related to you today by telephone.

We have just received the initial results of an interview conducted in Israel of Mr. Ivan Loboda. As you know Mr. Loboda and Ivan Shchedrov say they traveled to Laos in 1969. Mr. Loboda has said that he was present during an interview of your husband, David Hrdlicka, in the spring of 1969. He also reports that David appeared to be in good health at that time.

Obviously, this is a significant report, and we are taking numerous steps to follow up on this information. We will provide you with details about our efforts as soon as we can. Although we do not release information about an ongoing investigation until it is complete, I wanted to give you a "heads up" that we had received this information. Additionally, Mr. Loboda advised us he has received your letter and is planning to send you a response very shortly.

I assure you we will keep you apprised of our further efforts. We will relay any and all information we learn about your husband as soon as possible.

Sincerely,

Joe B. Harvey

Chief of Staff

Defense POW/MIA Office

CHAPTER 32

Viewing of David's Classified File

!996 Washington, D.C.

DPMO informed family members we could view our loved one's case file with a two-week notice. I called DPMO and made my request. In a few days, I received a call back stating there was no way they could have David's file ready.

"You stated that with a two-week notice family members can view their loved one's case file. I expect you to hold to your promise."

I knew that the reason for the two-week notice was so that DPMO could scrub the files and remove documents under the guise of sources and methods. They never wanted the families to get names so that we can initiate our own investigations.

I took David Jr. with me, and we spent three days going through the file with two people in the room watching us at all times. One was actually an analyst on David's case.

"What analytical qualifications and experience do you have to work on these files?" asked David, Jr.

The analyst responded, "Oh, I have no special training."

After we left the room, my son said to me, "Mom, when you are given a job to do, you are always briefed on how to do the job."

David, Jr. was a Naval fighter pilot. So, the issue that was supposed to be of **highest national priority was using untrained personnel!**

David Jr. was later told by Colonel Peck, who resigned from the DPMO in 1993, that the DIA was not looking for satellite imagery of POWs. As David Jr. and I read through his father's file, it became obvious there was no follow-up on the information, or at least there was none in the file. There was an evident lack of materials that should have been in an investigative file, such as radio intercepts, notes from interviews of individuals, or cables from CIA. As testified to by General Secord, "There should be a mountain of message traffic..." on the Hrdlicka case.

Amazingly, no government agency ever made an effort to interview the Russian reporter, Ivan Shchedrov, who interviewed David in captivity several times. That should really tell you everything you need to know.

I complained that the "Blood Chit" had been discontinued. Major Moore stated, "It has been reinstated," but years had been lost telling people who came forward with information that there was no reward for POWs. The CIA should have been tasked for information on David's case, since the CIA ran the war in Laos. But we know that that was never done.

David's Classified File Review

I asked if the DPMO had ever asked the CIA for reports on David's case. The answer was "no." That's very interesting, because with the CIA running the secret war in Laos, that is where most of the reports on David likely would have been found.

This is just another example of reports that concern live POWs being ignored. The DPMO has not done the very basic investigation, or the tasking of other government agencies like the CIA, to give them the information those agencies possess on the Hrdlicka case. The only conclusion I can come to is that the DPMO is not interested in doing a real investigation of live men. They are only interested if the individual is dead. Or, most likely, they are only interested in trying to make those who have survived many years in captivity dead.

CHAPTER 33

John McCain as Obstructionist to POWs/MIAs

1996

Senator John McCain was an obstructionist against the families of POW/MIAs for a long time. He clearly had no interest in getting at the truth. The question I had over the years for John McCain is WHY? Now, the question, since the passing of John McCain, who was a POW himself, is still WHY? The documents included in this book will show McCain started his obstruction as soon as he was elected to Congress. Then, there is the "1996 Hallway Meeting," where McCain showed the family members of a POW the contempt he had for all of us POW/MIA families. WHY? What reason did McCain have for setting himself up against POW/MIA families? I personally need to know.

We POW/MIA families were in the same position as his family during his captivity, just trying to protect our loved ones and get them returned. Families worked for six months getting the Missing Personnel Act passed into law. The Act had not been updated since 1942. The updated provisions were to protect future generations from having to endure the injustices the Vietnam Era families endured. In 1996, the following provisions to the POW/MIA Act were restored:

- Section 1502(a). Designates a period of no longer than 10 days for a unit commander to report to the theater commander that a person is missing.
- Section 1502(b). The theater commander, after receiving a report from a unit commander that a person is missing, has 14 days to forward a report to the Secretary concerned to ensure that all necessary actions were taken and all appropriate assets were used to resolve the status of the missing person, and that all pertinent information was safeguarded.
- Section 1505(b). For missing persons last known or suspected of being alive, a board of review will be convened every 3 years after the initial report of disappearance.
- Section 1506(c). Penalizes any government official who knowingly and willfully withholds information related to the disappearance, whereabouts, or status of a missing person from his case file.
- Section 1507. Prevents a missing service person from being declared dead without credible proof or requires that if a body is recovered and is not identifiable through visual means, a certification by a practitioner of an appropriate forensic science that the body recovered is the missing person.
- Section 1513(b). Permits civilian Defense Department employees who serve with or accompany the armed forces in the field under orders, who become missing as a result of hostile action to be covered by the Act.

On June 29, 1996, Jeannette Jenkins wrote a letter to the Senate Ethics Committee regarding the offensive behavior of Senator John McCain.

My name is Jeannette Jenkins. On June 20, 1996. I was with my husband Bill Jenkins and my Aunt, Jane Duke Gaylor, (mother of a POW). We were in the hall of the Senate Russell Building waiting to speak to Senator John McCain. There was a group of about 15 POW/MIA family members with us. We were attempting to hand deliver letters to Senator McCain requesting him to please drop his Amendment to the Missing Personnel Act. This Act was signed into law on February 10, 1996. Senator McCain came out of his office with a young woman and began walking towards our group. As he approached us, Carol Hrdlicka, wife of a POW, asked the Senator, "May we speak to you?" We did not rush towards him. Then John Parsels, a returned POW, asked him if he would take the letters. That is when McCain's face changed, and he became very angry. He then burst through our group shoving me with unreasonable force in a hostile manner. I was standing next to my Aunt who is in a wheelchair. Senator McCain did not give me the chance to get out of his way. His look was angry and hostile, and he shoved me without cause. All the Senator had to do was walk around me or at the very least given me the opportunity to get out of his way.

I feel Senator McCain's action of shoving me is reprehensible. His actions were unbecoming to a United States Senator. I immediately went to the Capitol police and reported the incident to Sgt. Dana Sundberg. I left my name and address with the Sgt., expecting him to make out an incident report. I have spoken to him twice since this time. He informed me that since this involved a Senator, I would have to speak to the Chief and file assault charges against the Senator. I told him that I wanted to seek legal advice because I really didn't understand what my rights were.

I feel it is a terrible shame when citizens cannot approach in a non-confrontational manner a United States Senator with concerns regarding an Amendment that Senator McCain is trying to pass, without being shoved by Senator McCain in the hall. The Senator did not even look back to see if I was injured.

Thank you for your assistance in this matter, and I am awaiting your response.

Sincerely,

Jeannette Jenkins

When the United States Government sends men into harm's way, they should do everything in their power to get the men in captivity released. The United States government has determined that our loved ones, who were known to be in captivity, were expendable for the "greater good" which turns out to be protecting the United States government from scrutiny. Senator John McCain led the way as long as he could, but the POW/MIA family members would not stand for it, although people who rely on regular news sources for their information are doubtless unaware of that fact. Right through his funeral and beyond, hardly any public figure in America has received a more favorable press than McCain.

* * *

Another letter regarding Senator McCain's behavior towards POW/MIA family members was sent to the Senate Ethics Committee on June 30, 1996.

> My name is Jane Duke Gaylor. My son, Charles Duke was abandoned in Vietnam. My niece and nephew, Bill and Jeannette Jenkins, were with me in the Senate Russell Building on June 20, 1996. We were there to deliver letters from POW/MIA family members to Senator John McCain in objection to his Amendment to the Missing Personnel Act, signed into law February 10, 1996. The family members had worked very diligently to get this Act passed. This is the first new legislation since 1942. We, as family members, have an unequivocal interest and great concern in this Act because of our loved ones. We and our missing loved ones are the victims of this mishandled tragedy. We as family members object to Senator McCain's Amendment to repeal The Missing Personnel Act.
>
> We were in a group of about 15 family members, as Senator John McCain came out of his office with a young lady. John Parsels, a returned POW, asked Senator McCain to take the letters. Upon Mr. Parsels request, the Senator burst forward in a running walk with a very angry look. He then said, "I do not know what you are

talking about. I do not know anything about the Missing Personnel Act." I was in a wheelchair and my niece was standing next to me. Senator McCain then shoved my niece hard in a very hostile manner, not caring what harm it could have caused her. He acted in a very violent manner. His reckless disregard for the impact on my niece, who had been in the emergency room the night before because of a migraine headache, was very unethical in his position as a United States Senator. I will not have my niece abused by any irresponsible government authority – not even Senator John McCain.

His act of abuse was reported to Sgt. Dana Sundberg of the Capital Police, who advised her of the need to file assault charges against the Senator. My niece informed him that she wanted to seek legal advice before filing charges.

I am asking for your response to these unethical actions of Senator John McCain.

Thank you and God Bless

Jane Duke Gaylor

Mother of alive POW in Vietnam

* * *

There were several more letters to the Senate Ethics Committee from family members of POW/MIA present in the hallway and witness to Senator John McCain's physical abuse of Jeannette Jenkins on that day.

I wrote the following letter on the 8th of July 1996 to the Senate Ethics Committee:

I wish to file a complaint against Senator John McCain and want Senator McCain sanctioned for behavior unbecoming a United States Senator. I am attaching a Statement of what took place and why Senator McCain should be sanctioned. I personally have viewed the Senator taking time out in the halls of the Senate to be photographed with visitors, so why was he so abusive to family members of POW/MIA when we approached the Senator to ask his support on legislation that is important to the families?

Senator McCain denied knowing The Missing Personnel Act when he, himself, has introduced an Amendment to the very Act. I ask you, is that an ethical way for a Senator to act when approached and questioned about his own legislation? Would it not have been more respectful for the Senator to at least have accepted the letters written by family members asking for his support of our men? Instead, he refused to accept the letters, became hostile and angry, pushing a young lady aside in a hasty exit.

I proceeded to follow McCain stating we just wanted him to leave the Missing Personnel Act alone.

Again, McCain stated, "I don't know about any Missing Personnel Act."

By this time, we had reached the elevator, and he was frantically looking up at the elevator hoping the doors would open.

He turned and said to me, "You don't know what I've been through."

I answer, "Yes I do, and David Hrdlicka is still going through it."

I have the capture picture in a badge, and I hold it up for McCain to see. I notice that McCain's face is red and sweating.

At that moment, the Senator's elevator arrives, and he quickly steps on (the public is not supposed to use the Senator's elevator).

He then states to me, "You just don't understand."

I state back to him, "Yes I do, and you're a traitor."

At that point, the elevator doors shut so I run down the stairs trying to catch up, but he has disappeared. Later that day, I saw him down the hall in the Capitol Building, and when he saw me, he turned around and disappeared again.

> Is there no decency and respect left in the Senate for the very people they are supposed to represent? There was a family member from Arizona accompanying our group, Eleanor Apodaca, sister of Major Victor Apodaca, MIA. Our group approached Senator McCain in a very quiet, non-confrontational manner. Senator McCain's abusive behavior towards American citizens should not be tolerated by his fellow Senators. We were, after all, asking for his help for men who are still possibly lingering in captivity. Wouldn't you think Senator McCain, of all people, would be sympathetic to someone who may still be held prisoner in Vietnam?
>
> Sincerely,
>
> Carol Hrdlicka
>
> Wife of Col. David L. Hrdlicka
>
> Known to be Alive in Captivity

As the "Hall Confrontation" occurred June 20,1996, out of the flurry of letters that followed John McCain's confrontational abuse of Jeannette Jenkins, there is one letter that stands out in stating the unforgivable repercussions that resulted from Senator McCain's behavior. The letter was dated July 28, 1996, from Roger Hall, again, to the Senate Select Committee on Ethics:

> On Thursday June 20, 1996, I was present when Senator John McCain approached a group of POW/MIA family members after coming out of an office in the Russell Office Building, and as he approached, he broke out in a big smile. John Parsels, a former POW, asked the Senator to accept some letters from POW/MIA family members. Senator McCain's expression changed instantly to that of anger and he said, "No." Carol Hrdlicka stepped forward and asked to speak to him about the Missing Persons Act and Senator McCain said he didn't "know anything about it" and burst forward with deliberate disregard for anyone standing in his way. It was necessary for me to quickly step back to keep from being

overrun by him. The POW/MIA family members were on Senator McCain's right side of the hallway. He could have easily walked around them without any difficulty.

Senator McCain, followed by his assistant, pushed into Mrs. Jeannette Jenkins with his arm because she was in his way. That Mrs. Jenkins did not react quickly enough to get out of John McCain's way is no reason for him to have pushed his way so aggressively. Mrs. Jenkins was recovering from migraine headaches that required emergency treatment the night before...(avoiding repetition of other letters).

The situation so aggravated Ms. Gaylor's poor health that it was necessary to place her in a nursing home. Ms. Gaylor has informed that Walter Lehman of Senator McCain's office has attempted to deceive her by insisting that the McCain Amendment was passed in April, when it is still in Committee. Mr. Lehman has also tried to embarrass her about going to Senator McCain with her concerns on June 20th, stating he "can't believe that she would admit being with those people." It is terrible when American citizens with an equity interest in legislation cannot address a United States Senator about an Amendment he is sponsoring in committee without being assaulted and lied to by the Senator and his staff. This is not the first incident where Senator McCain has abused POW/MIA family members. John McCain should be sanctioned for his acts.

There was never any reply to the letters sent about this event. No attempt to rectify.

The only indirect result to rectify the above damages to POW/MIA family members by Senator John McCain came from Tom Davis, Member of Congress addressed to the attention of Colonel John R. Niemela dated

August 20, 1996.

Dear Colonel Niemela:

Thank you for your letter regarding deletion of the Missing Personnel Act provisions of the FY 1997 National Defense Authorization Act. I appreciate hearing from you.

It may interest you to know that I am a cosponsor of H.R. 4000 sponsored by Rep. Bob Dornan (R-Ca) which would restore the provisions of Chapter 76 of that title (relating to missing persons) that were deleted from the 1997 Defense Authorization bill. The bill has 255 cosponsors and has been referred to the National Security Committee.

As you may know, Senator John McCain (R-AZ) got the Missing In Action (MIA) provisions of the Defense Authorization bill deleted during conference. These provisions were part of the House defense bill that was sent to conference with the Senate to work out differences between the two bills. It was during this conference that Senator McCain, a Senate appointed conferee as a senior member of the Senate Armed Services Committee acted to gut the provisions dealing with MIAs. Normally, a senator on the Armed Services Committee could get these provisions modified in committee or offer an amendment in the Senate to make changes they want. This would have required a Senate vote in committee or on the floor of the Senate. It is unusual for a member of Congress to wait till committee and then insist on substantive changes to passed legislation, however, that is what happened in this case.

The FY 1997 Defense Authorization bill has passed the House by an overwhelming margin. For that reason, Rep. Dornan has offered a separate, free-standing bill to restore these provisions. It is my hope that we can move quickly to bring this bill to the floor for passage. There appears to be overwhelming support in the House for the bill. However, I would note that Senator McCain could place substantial obstacles in the way of this legislation in the Senate if he chooses to.

Be assured that I will be following this legislation closely and working for its passage. Again, thank you for writing, and I hope that you will continue to let me know how you feel about this or any other issue of importance to you.

Sincerely,

Tom Davis

Member of Congress

* * *

FACT SHEET: SENATOR JOHN MCCAIN

Prepared by Patricia O'Grady, Ph.D. August 1996
Live POW Committee/National League of Families of POWS/MIAS

1. **SENATOR JOHN MCCAIN** demonstrated a **CONFLICT OF INTEREST.**

During his tenure as Vice-Chair of the Senate Select Committee on POWs/MIAs and should have recused himself from the deliberations;

2. **SENATOR JOHN MCCAIN DISTORTED HIS POW WAR RECORD** and, in fact, acted as a collaborator for which he received special treatment while a POW. Special treatment included a large private cell with windows while detained at 17 Ly Nam De Street in Hanoi. Senator John McCain refuses to release his POW debriefings to the public which would substantiate his true activity, behavior, and decorum as a POW. Instead, Senator McCain passed legislation, the Privacy

Act of 1992, to ensure that these damaging documents would remain in secrecy. As a public official, who trades on his heroic POW record, Senator McCain should be compelled to release his debriefings immediately to the American public;

3. The Vietnamese maintained an independent set of records on each POW. These files are

Known as the "V" Files or the "Blue" Files. **SENATOR JOHN MCCAIN** has gone on record **stating that the files should not be released** because some of the returned POWs would be "embarrassed" by the "silly" things reported therein. ***
Critics claim that the release of these files are critical to the resolution of many POW / MIA Cases.

4. SENATOR JOHN MCCAIN'S official position is that NO AMERICAN POWS/MIAS WERE LEFT BEHIND in Southeast Asia in 1973 despite findings to the contrary by his own Senate Select Committee; and that no American POWS / MIAs still survive despite compelling evidence to the contrary;
5. SENATOR JOHN MCCAIN has treated dozens of POW and MIA family members with RUDENESS, ARROGANCE, INSENSITIVITY, AND DISRESPECT on numerous occasions.

National Security Committee, Military Personnel Subcommittee
Statement of Carol Hrdlicka
September 10, 1996

Mr. Chairman and Committee Members, thank you for inviting me to give testimony before this Committee. I am very concerned about the McCain Amendment which in essence made the Missing

Service Personnel Act ineffective in the protection of our men who are sent into harm's way. This legislation had not been changed since 1942. I would think with all the advanced technology it should have been updated.

I would like to know the rationale behind Senator McCain's changes. Let's just go through the changes and if anyone here can explain how these changes offer **more protection** to the men who are sent into harm's way, I would appreciate your input. I am mystified why Senator McCain, of all people, **is not interested** in protecting our men **now and in the future.**

Section 1502(a) changes the time period to report someone missing from 48 hours to 10 days. In the civilian community you are reported missing after 24 hours. If Senator McCain had the misfortune to have landed in the jungle with his broken arms, would he have minded waiting 10 days to be reported missing? How can this be of benefit to our service members?

Section 1502(b) has unit commanders reporting directly to the appropriate Service Secretary. Is the Service Secretary going to be in the combat theatre or sitting in the Pentagon in Washington D.C.? How will that benefit our service members. Does an investigating detective sit in his office and go to the scene of the crime?

Section 1505(b) change review boards from three years until there is new information. In many cases there **has been new information** that has not been relayed to the families. At the present time government agencies and their personnel have a license to lie to the families under the guise that men have to be sacrificed for the good of the "greater good." I would like to know, for what **"greater good" David L. Hrdlicka has been sacrificed?**

Section 1506(b) changes the penalization of any government official who knowingly and willfully withholds information of a missing person. Don't future generations deserve better treatment than the families have received in the past? Should we be asked to sacrifice our loved ones and never know the truth about their fate? Would any of you be willing to sacrifice your children, brothers, sisters, or any member of your family and never know what happened to them? Why shouldn't the people in charge of government agencies be held accountable?

Section 1507 repeal of the requirement that a person can be declared dead (3) without credible proof (4) that a body or remains have to have certification by a practitioner or appropriate forensic science if a body can't be identified by visual means. Would you be willing to accept pig bones in the place of your family member? Would you be willing to have your family member declared dead with no credible proof? Is there no **common sense or logic** left in Washington? How can you ask us, as family members, to accept such a **degrading practice** for our loved ones?

Section 1513 takes away the rights of DOD civilian contract employees to be covered by the Act. Why shouldn't the civilian employees have the right to be accounted for if they become missing during a military operation?

What **possible rationale** could there be for the above changes. I would personally like to hear Senator McCain's own explanation. What agenda could Senator McCain possibly have to "**strip**" the Missing Service Personnel Act of all its protection for service members who could possibly end up in captivity as he did? Why would Senator McCain want to protect men **who have lied to the families?**

A group of family members tried to hand letters to Senator McCain to ask that he not make these changes and he refused to accept our letters. Senator McCain stated on the Senate floor that the families and the veterans agreed with his Amendment. Nothing could be further from the truth – in other words, that is a **LIE.** Senator McCain does not speak for the families nor does he care what we want. Senator McCain won't even meet with the families or accept our letters. "CINCs don't have time to worry about lieutenants or sergeants." Does that mean, lieutenants or sergeants **are not important?** Maybe the CINCs should be on the front lines.

Why is it that Senator McCain **supports** anything the Vietnamese communists want – for instance, lifting of the trade embargo, normalization, or most favored nation? Yet, Senator McCain's voting record shows a lack of support on many of the American veterans issues or our abandoned POWs! Why would a former **pow hug his former captor?** I believe Senator McCain's **"Achille's heel"** reveals his behavior during his captivity.

There is much arguing as to who is to **blame** in the POW issue – well, I believe there is enough blame for everyone to share, **both Democratic and Republican.** Let's just look at the record of the Presidents over the years: First, we have Johnson who escalated the war; then we have Nixon who got on television and lied about all the POWs being home; then we have Carter who declared all the men dead with no credible evidence; then we have Reagan, who meant well, but was surrounded by people who **did not want the POW "can of worms" exposed,** so he refused the offer to buy the USG 57 POWs in 1981; then there was Bush who knew the **whole truth** as a former CIA Director and could have asked the Vietnamese to return our men but didn't; and, finally, we have Clinton, who was a draft dodger and protester who does not like the military, so he also turned a blind eye to the plight of our men. As you can see, both sides are well represented, Democrat and Republican.

We have heard for 23 years how the POW issue is the **Highest National Priority.** If that is the case, why haven't the cases where the men were known to be alive in captivity been solved? In 1992 the Senate Select Committee, finally after 19 years, admitted men had been left behind in captivity in Vietnam.

Allow me to give you my view on DPMO's investigation on my husband's case. My son and I viewed the "classified file" DPMO has on my husband, David L. Hrdlicka, in May of this year. This "classified file" is nothing more than a record of their own feeble attempts **at what they call investigating.** The DPMO hires underachievers and buries them in paperwork. There is no effort to investigate leads unless you actually show the DPMO "**the lead.**" Example: There was no effort made to contact the Russian reporter who **interviewed** David several times in captivity. This last December of 1995, I asked if they had ever made such an effort – the answer was **"no."** Then, the DPMO began their **1996 investigation,** some 30 years late. The DPMO will now have to re-think their position that David died in 1968. David was seen alive in **1969** at a press conference in the caves of Laos (read DPMO Letter). Of course, there is no evidence to back up the DPMO 1968 date, just their **assumption.** DPMO is nothing more than a data dump.

The DPMO has not even made a request for the cables referring to a rescue attempt that was testified to by General Secord where he states, "There should be a raft of cables in the CIA."

Why hasn't the DPMO requested those cables? During our three-day viewing of David's classified file, one of the analysts admitted he had no special training in the analytical field. Is that the way investigations are done? Hire people who have no experience and let them **learn or not learn** on the job? Does this sound like "HIGHEST NATIONAL PRIORITY?"

In 1992 I sent a Freedom of Information to the Defense Intelligence Agency requesting all documents pertaining to rescue attempts for David and specifically requested anything on the code name of "Duck Soup." I received a response on 10 August 1992 from Mr. Charles Trowbridge denying any rescue attempts were made for David. (Read Trowbridge letter & Duck Soup documents). I have received the deposition of Thomas Moorer from a researcher wherein it addresses a rescue operation in 1972 to rescue approximately 60 American POWs held in Laos. Now, I will have to assume someone is **lying**. Is it Casualty? Or could it be Mr. Trowbridge is deliberately lying, and if so, **WHY?**

In the beginning, the Air Force Casualty did not send any documents to me. They just kept me informed by telephone and letter. I was informed in 1966 there had been a rescue attempt, but they were not sure whether they had Hrdlicka or Shelton. Whichever man it was, was recaptured. Now, I will have to conclude, that if what Mr. Trowbridge says is true, and there were **no rescue attempts** for David, then Air Force Casualty was **lying to me from the beginning.** You must be informed that Mr. Charles Trowbridge has made a career out of the POW issue. I have reports as early as 1966 with Mr. Trowbridge's signature on the bottom. Mr. Trowbridge says **I can go** to the Library of Congress and get the information on David's case – I would like to know – **as a taxpayer,** what they have done with the budget they have had for over 30 years. **I should not have to spend my limited resources on investigating David's case –** that is what Mr. Trowbridge has been **paid to do for years.**

Mr. Trowbridge seems to have difficulty telling the truth! During the Senate Select Committee Hearings Senator Bob Smith wanted to call Trowbridge a "**Liar**" in public. You can **candy coat** what Mr. Trowbridge has done any way you want and call it misrepresentation or misinformation. But I call it what it is – **Lies!** I do understand that my husband and the other men left behind are expendable by Mr. Trowbridge's standards, or lack thereof, and that is just the **cost** of war in his eyes. Mr. Trowbridge is under an umbrella that gives him the authority to lie to Congress and me, as a family member. With all this in mind, do you think Mr. Trowbridge should be rehired to continue his career off the backs of POWs and MIAs?

During the period of time after Col. Peck resigned from the DIA, Trowbridge filled in until a replacement could be found. On one occasion, my son, David M., was visiting me and wanted to know who the U.S. Postal worker was who was referenced in a 1990 letter from DIA stating Col. David L. Hrdlicka had tried to escape. We then placed a call to Mr. Trowbridge and put the question to him. During the conversation, Mr. Trowbridge suggested my son come to see him in person at which time he indicated he would give my son the name of the postal worker. When I son arrived, Trowbridge backtracked. He then made a statement that there may not have been a postal worker. After repeated attempts to get the original report this letter was taken from, a researcher found a report, **which I believe the letter was taken from.** However, **it does not mention a postal worker, but says information came from a Federal Agent.** If that is the case, why did Mr. Trowbridge misinterpret the facts? .The "Frenchman" referred to in the letter – (Mr. Trowbridge couldn't be sure of the name), may have been Pierre O'Reilly. At that time Mr. Trowbridge was the Deputy Chief of POW/MIA in the Defense Intelligence Agency, and he isn't sure who a source is? That does not give me a great deal of confidence in the intelligence gathering capabilities of the DIA.

This should be a good example why the families can no longer trust the individuals in these agencies and the need for drastic changes. We need legislation that will give us power to get at the truth. How is it, that in February 1996, we were able to get the Missing Personnel Act passed into law and by August, we had that law totally "**gutted**!" There have been many committees on the problems, but there is never any follow-up **action.** We, as families, have been **promised** time and again there will be **action!** I would liken the **promises of Washington to a Barnum & Bailey Circus.** Just entertainment for the public benefit but no substance – I mean no disrespect to Barnum & Bailey.

Thank you,

Carol Hrdlicka

CHAPTER 34

No Resolution to the POWs/MIAs Abandoned in Laos

I met Roger Hall in 1993. As a researcher, he was instrumental in finding many of the documents on David's case in the archives which I had never received from either DPMO or DIA. His extremely informative article, "Abandoned in Laos," appeared in the January-February 1997 issue of the *U.S. Veteran Dispatch*. It is reprinted in full below:

> American POWs known to have been held captive by the communist Pathet Lao (PL) were abandoned in Laos in 1973. When the United States withdrew the last of our fighting forces from Vietnam on March 28, 1973, Americans that were then prisoners from secret operations in Laos during the Vietnam War were abandoned to the Lao Patriotic Front (LPF), the political group of whom the Pathet Lao were the fighting forces. This was the result, not the intent, of withdrawing U.S. troops under the Paris Peace Agreement (PPA) to secure the release of the named POWs; it is also the result of not negotiating with the LPF for prisoners they held, in the mistaken belief that North Vietnam would deliver them to us.
>
> The Laotians have made proving that Americans are in captivity there difficult at best and seemingly impossible under international law. The communists are masters at keeping and hiding American POWs. They have it down to a science. At the suspicion

that a location was known or would become known because of an escape or for any other reason, American prisoners would be moved. Prisoners were held in the most secure areas where they were under heavy guard by troops. They were usually held in caves that also served military functions where they could be hidden, controlled, and protected from recovery.

No one captured by the Pathet Lao during the war was ever released. Only two Americans escaped and were recovered from the Pathet Lao during the Vietnam War. Navy Lt. Charles Klussman, shot down on June 6, 1964 over the Plain of Jars, Laos, had the fortunate distinction of being the first POW to escape from the Pathet Lao. Navy Pilot Dieter Dengler, shot down on February 2, 1965, was captured by the Pathet Lao and held prisoner with two Americans – Gene Debruin, a civilian, and Lt. Duane Martin, a helicopter pilot. Martin was reported by Dengler as possibly killed while evading after the escape. President Nixon in 1973 was under great pressure from the U.S. Congress, the POW/MIA family members, and the public to bring the war to an end and have the POWs released. Congress had passed the Cooper-Church Amendment that cut off all funding for further military action, which prevented enforcement of the Paris Peace Agreement.

Due to the public's demand to end the war, delayed release of the known POWs was not a risk that the administration decision makers were likely to take. No one informed the Congress or the American people that there were captives that had not been released from Southeast Asia and turned its back on the POWs in Laos. As the years passed from 1973, the fate of these individuals seemingly became less and less important.

The Secret War in Laos

The United States fought a secret war in Laos against the communist Pathet Lao in support of the Royal Laotian Government (RLG) from 1962 through 1973. Laos was in the North Vietnamese (DRV) theater of operations, where the North Vietnamese and Pathet Lao fought battles against the U.S.-supported noncommunist Laotians. Under the 1962 Geneva Agreement, both the U.S. and the North Vietnamese were obliged not to be in Laos.

This secret war was managed by the military role of the CIA out of the American Embassy in Vientiane, Laos, under the authority of the U.S. Ambassador. Presidential authority gave the ambassador right to manage and conduct military operations that included U.S. military aircraft and personnel but excluded the U.S. military from any decision-making in their use. The separate though interrelated bombing of the Ho Chi Minh Trail that bordered Vietnam, Hanoi's pipeline of supply to their forces in South Vietnam, was under the control of the Military Assistance Command Vietnam (MACV).

The Paris Peace Agreement was signed on January 27, 1973 and the names of POWs captured in Vietnam were given to U.S. representatives. On February 1, U.S. negotiators exchanged a letter from President Nixon agreeing to pay the Vietnamese $3.25 billion in reconstruction and in return for the unnegotiated "Laos List" of names of American POWs captured in Laos who were to be released. The $3.25 billion was for reconstruction in Vietnam. There was no consideration for Laos.

Although North Vietnamese forces controlled over 85% of the territory in Laos where Americans were missing in action and had advisors attached to all Pathet Lao units, the list handed over by the North Vietnamese contained the names of only nine Americans and one Canadian POW captured in Laos and held by the DRV in Hanoi. These were the only POWs from Laos to be released. There was "a firm and unequivocal understanding that all American prisoners in Laos will be released within 60 days of the signing of the Vietnam Agreement."

The U.S. knew that the Pathet Lao had information on many of the American POW/MIA in Laos. Of the 10 POWs released under the Vietnam Agreement, none were from Pathet Lao POW camps, and the Pathet Lao insisted that they held prisoners in Laos that would be released by themselves. The fighting between the Royal Laotian Government and Pathet Lao ended when the Laos ceasefire was signed by the Laotian Parties in Vientiane on February 21, 1973. The Agreement stated that 60 days after the coalition government was formed all POWs would be released. This was the fallback agreement the U.S. hoped to use to have U.S. POWs held in Laos released. This was in addition to the Paris Peace Accords.

The Pathet Lao were under the direct military supervision of their communist North Vietnamese cadres, even more so than the South Vietnamese, and the Royal Laotian Government were under the influence of the United States. During the peace negotiations, Henry Kissinger had insisted that the Vietnamese be responsible for all prisoners in Southeast Asia. This has been one of the points Le Duc Tho, the North Vietnamese negotiator, would not agree to, claiming that Laos was a sovereign nation and would be responsible for their own prisoners. Although the North Vietnamese did then and possibly now influence the POW/MIA policy of Laos, efforts for the release of known POWs from the Pathet Lao failed.

Record Tracking of U.S. POWs in Laos

Vietnam War era CIA reports state that American POWs captured in Northern Laos are "escorted to prisons in Houa Phan/Sam Nuea/province where they are detained on a semi-permanent basis or transferred to North Vietnam." What follows here are reports of Pathet Lao held POWs in the Laotian theater of operations and this does not include the MACV area of operations in Laos. The Pathet Lao held American POWs in numerous locations, including the Pathet Lao Headquarters at Sam Nuea and at more than one location at Ban Nakay. Declassified CIA documents from 1967-1972 show that there were up to 60 or more U.S. POWs held by the Pathet Lao during the Vietnam War who were never released.

Reports entitled "Enemy Prisons in Laos," "Estimated Enemy Prison Facilities in Laos," and "Estimated Enemy Prison Order of Battle in Laos" provide information from sources on communist Pathet Lao POW camps holding prisoners described as pilots, Caucasian and American. Reports were updated as new intelligence was obtained.

There is also a 1969 Seventh Air Force report "POW Camps Listing for Laos," describing "all locations listed have been validated for inclusion by appropriate authority at the U.S. Embassy in Vientiane in coordination with the Joint Personnel Recovery Center (JPRC)." The JPRC was responsible for the reporting and tracking of all missing and captured Americans under the code name "BRIGHT LIGHT." Another report, the "1972 Fleet Intelligence Center Pacific, Laos Prisoner of War Camp Study," is a compilation of overhead photographic imagery of all known POW

Camps in Laos. These two reports incorporated the CIA intelligence products and were backed up with the original source reports.

Known and Suspected POWs Under Pathet Lao Control: (Listed by year, organization, and Number of POWs).

1966 – CIA – 8 American POWs

1967 – CIA – 15 American POWs

1968 – CIA - 13 American POWs

1969 - CIA - 45 American POWs

1969 - USAF 61 American POWs

1970 - CIA - 28-30 American POWs

1971 - CIA - 24-30 American POWs

1972 - NAVY high altitude photography of known and suspected POW Camps in Laos was not released.

CIA POW/MIA reporting decreased after 1969. This was at a time when the military was still losing aircraft and pilots and others, both civilian and military, were being lost on the ground. Many POW camps had been observed for long periods of time, some for years. On March 11, 1968, the communists attacked a U.S. Tactical Air Navigation System (TACAN) and a TSQ 81 Radar bomb facility at Phu Pha Thi, also known as Lima Site 85, in northern Laos. General Singkapo, the former Commander of all Pathet Lao Forces during the war is quoted in an August 21, 1990 interview with Dr. Timothy Castle, author of *At War in the Shadow of Vietnam*, as saying that "About 100 Pathet Lao and more than 200 North Vietnamese…attacked" Lima Site 85 and that "Some two or three Americans were captured at the site and sent to Vietnam." Also, in 1968, reports were received by the CIA in Laos that all American POWs were being sent to Hanoi for a prisoner exchange. Twenty-seven Americans that were held prisoner by the Pathet Lao in four different POW camps were moved to Ban Hang Long, Houa Phan Province, and were supposed to represent all Americans held by the Pathet Lao, CIA POW reporting shown above indicates not all were sent.

On October 11, 1969, overhead photography taken by an air-breathing drone reconnaissance aircraft [Project Buffalo Hunter] of Ban Nakay Teu revealed 20 non-Asians accompanied by Pathet Lao guards near caves at Ban Nakay Teu." CIA analysis of the prisoners determined them to be Caucasian. There had been numerous ground reports identifying these people as Americans both prior to and after the overhead reconnaissance.

In 1971, Secretary of Defense Laird was not satisfied with the limited information he was receiving on the POWs in Laos. He sent General Vessey to Laos to assist in operations there and offer military intelligence assets in the gathering of POW/MIA information. Ambassador Godley refused the offer of military intelligence assistance and informed DOD that all POW reporting requirements could be handled by the embassy.

President Nixon was notified by Henry Kissinger at the White House on March 19, 1973, that "The U.S. Embassy in Vientiane has been told by the Pathet Lao that the U.S. prisoners of war in Laos will be released by the Lao Communists in Laos and not by the Vietnamese in Hanoi."

On March 22, Ambassador Godley cabled the Secretary of State and the White House that "We believe the LPF holds throughout Laos more prisoners than are found on the DRV lists...We do not believe it is reasonable to expect the LPF to be able to produce an accurate total POW list by March 28; the LPF just has not focused on the POW repatriation and accounting problem until very recently and probably cannot collect in the next few days, the information we require." It was realized, based on the number of people known to have been alive on the ground and captured, that additional prisoners should be released from Laos. Admiral Moorer, on President Nixon's authority, ordered a halt to the troop withdrawal because the Pathet Lao had not released any of the expected POW/MIAs. The next day the Four Party Joint Military Commission (FPJMC) informed the White House to get the nine out now and we would get the rest later, that "a bird in the hand was worth two in the bush." President Nixon reversed his decision, and the troop withdrawal was resumed.

The White House memorandum for the President of March 24, 1973, from Henry Kissinger included the statement of the Chief North Vietnamese Delegate that "The question of military personnel captured in Laos can in no way be associated with the Paris

Peace Agreement and withdrawal of U.S. troops." This should have been noted as a sign that the North Vietnamese were not going to adhere to their responsibility for all POWs in southeast Asia as the President and the public had been informed. Although the Pathet Lao had insisted that "prisoners captured in Laos would be returned in Laos," the nine Americans and one Canadian whose names were on the Laos list were released at Gia Lam Airport in Hanoi on 28 March 1973. The head of the Pathet Lao delegation, Lt. Col. Thoong Sing, was present for the release of the POWs. The LPF must have been amazed, if not offended, at the refusal of the United States to seriously negotiate with them.

The withdrawal of U.S. troops was also completed on March 28th. Our military strength was down to 5,300 troops as of March 22nd. The North Vietnamese had left 10 divisions in South Vietnam and had been bringing a continuous flow of troops and supplies down the Ho Chi Minh Trail, in violation of the Paris Peace Accords.

Ambassador Godley had never spoken to the Pathet Lao spokesman Sot Petrasy, who had the rank of Ambassador. He had repeatedly stated the Pathet Lao were not to be believed and were just lackeys of the Vietnamese, a very severe approach to have taken with those who were holding American prisoners.

Ambassador Godley accepted the Pathet Lao statement that all POWs captured in Laos had been released to suit his requirements for the troop withdrawal and POW release under the Paris accords. The quick acceptance of the new Pathet Lao claim was in complete contradiction of the American embassy's stated 10-year position that the Pathet Lao could not be believed and would make political statements to suit their needs.

General Secord stated in his testimony before the Senate Select Committee on POW/MIA Affairs (SSC) in 1992 that CIA and other prison camp reports were not considered in Ambassador Godley's attempts to inquire of American POWs in Laos. The tracking by the CIA of Americans believed held captive in Laos was an ongoing task at the Embassy. The fact of Americans being held was known; the problem was where – for, prisoners were moved. Although some prisoners were held at a specific location, it may not have been possible to identify specific individuals at each site. In spite of the known captivity of POWs such as Hrdlicka, Shelton, Debruin and the POW camp reporting of 20-60 captive Americans, the lack of positive identification of POWs at specific coordinates was the deciding factor to accept the 10 POWs from Laos held in Hanoi and proceed with the prisoner exchange and troop withdrawal.

David Hrdlicka, shot down on May 18, 1965, had made public statements that were published in Pathet Lao newspapers and broadcast on Pathet Lao radio. Charles Shelton was downed on April 29, 1965. These two men were known to be held together in a cave southeast of Sam Nuea, Laos. In a rescue attempt of the two, one of them made it to a recovery area before being recaptured. Eugene Debruin escaped with Dieter Dengler but was separated, and his fate remains unknown.

The war had been fought to decide who would rule in Laos. A U.S. decision, after the signing of the Lao cease fire, to "not complicate" Lao negotiations with the U.S. POW issue proved wrong. Since March 1971, "The United States Government has scrupulously refrained from introducing complicating issues such as American POWs" into the Lao internal talks. The U.S. requested in 1972 that Souvana Phouma inquire about our POWs, but the RLG were just the lackeys of the United States "interventionists."

Admiral Moorer informed the chief delegate of the FPJMC in Saigon on March 23rd that "We intend to pursue the question of other U.S. personnel captured or missing in Laos following the release of the men on the February list." Unfortunately, the LPF were not members of the Commission for the recovery of American MIAs as were North Vietnam and the Viet Cong.

The captives held by the Pathet Lao in Laos were left without further efforts for their release because Congress had cut off funding for further action in Southeast Asia. There was no way to enforce our demands and the communists knew it. Congress was not informed of the captive Americans from the secret war who were thought to have been sent to fight in Vietnam.

President Nixon, on March 29, 1973, stated on national television that "All of our POWs are on their way home." On April 12, Deputy Assistant Secretary of Defense Roger Shields announced that "DOD had no specific knowledge indicating that any U.S. personnel were still alive and held prisoner in Southeast Asia." These two announcements signaled the end of the release of POWs under the Paris Peace Accords.

On May 18th, Admiral Zumwalt, the Chief of Naval Operations (CNO) informed Admiral Thomas Moorer, the Chairman, Joint Chief of Staff (CJCS) that the Laotians' inability to reach political agreements "has effectively arrested any movement toward an environment in which the status of Americans missing in action in Laos can be resolved. I am informed that the Central Intelligence Agency is pursuing a 'highest priority effort' directed at specifically determining what has happened to U.S. MIAs in Laos...In view of the direct and personnel interest the Services have in this matter, I recommend that the JCS receive a briefing from the CIUA on their effort in this area so that we may be confident this important humanitarian issue is receiving appropriate attention."

Lt. Gen. Deane, Jr., USA Acting Director of the Defense Intelligence Agency [DIA], advised Admiral Moorer at the time that "the CIA collection effort in Laos is carried out by the [CIA] assets, and within the organizational structure of the CIA station in Laos...DIA is collaborating closely where appropriate with CIA in regard to the current situation in Laos. A summary of the present POW/MIA situation in Laos as held in DIA files is as follows: (a) At present there are approximately 215 lost under such circumstances that the Patriotic Laotian Front (PLF) probably has information regarding their fate (b) Previous PLF mention of U.S. POWs detained in Laos includes a statement on 3 October 1967, by the Pathet Lao Radio, that between 17 May and 16 September 1967, the Pathet Lao had 'captured about a dozen U.S. pilots.' Furthermore, on 2 February 1971, PLF spokesman Sot Petrasy commended that, "'quelques dixaines' ('some tens') of prisoners were being held by the Pathet Lao...the PLF has provided no accounting for U.S. personnel in its custody." The DIA was the lead POW/MIA agency and recommended that the JCS not be briefed on the covert CIA activities. The briefing never occurred. On Wednesday, May 23, 1973, Kissinger, and Le Duc Tho agreed that, while not stating acceptance on the U.S. statement that Article 8(b) [POW/MIAs] applied to all of Indochina, Le Duc Tho would not contradict him publicly either. In return, the U.S. would not hold Vietnam to this because Vietnam had to cooperate with their Lao friends. This side-agreement has complicated negotiations in Laos to this very day.

Then a June 9th White House memorandum from the situation room informed Henry Kissinger that "The Pathet Lao chief representative in Vientiane...told our Embassy officer that further information on two ... acknowledged POWs (Hrdlicka and Debruin) must await the formation of a new coalition government in Laos."

In June 1973, a White House message from Henry Kissinger to the American Embassy Charge d'Affairs Dean stated "Le Duc Tho complained to me last week that you had mentioned US-DRV understanding regarding U.S. prisoners captured in Laos in your talk with Phoumi Vongvichit. We obviously cannot afford to give Hanoi this sort of grounds on which to abort their understanding with us."

The evidence that Americans were held in Laos was known at the time; however, it just wasn't considered in negotiations. The National Security Council, Washington Special Action Group (WSAG) headed by Henry Kissinger, received POW information from the CIA, the State Department, and the DOD, who were all members of the WSAG. But the U.S. Government had a timetable to keep for withdrawal of American fighting forces from Southeast Asia by March 28th under the Paris Peace Accords and the recovery of the reported Americans was put off for possible later efforts that never materialized.

The accepted loss of captured members of the U.S. Armed Forces and civilians by members of the U.S. Government is beyond comprehension, but it did happen. The 27 American prisoners and other American POWs reportedly sent to North Vietnam, seem also to have disappeared. They were not among the POWs on the February 1st, 1973 Laos list who were never returned. Those who were returned had been captured from 1965 through 1972 and most were moved to North Vietnam at different times. **The rest were withheld.** (emphasis added)

There were unusual situations in the 1968-69 time frame that could have had a bearing on the POWs' fate. A possible prisoner exchange may have been in process, and these men were never put into the known Vietnamese prison system. That year, Richard Nixon became President and Ho Chi Minh died. The POWs could have been executed. However, they could also have been sent to the U.S.S.R. for third-country internment and/or technical exploitation.

There are reports of prisoners being transferred to other communist countries throughout the war period. One source of such reports was Jerry Mooney, a former Air Force/NSA analyst who tracked POWs moved through Vietnam and Laos and sent to Russia. The NSA had tracked POWs in Laos throughout the war and until 1975 when U.S. intelligence assets were pulled out.

Former Czech General Jan Sejna, who defected from communist Czechoslovakia [and now works for DIA], has firsthand knowledge that close to 100 Americans in good physical condition were transferred from Vietnam to Russia via Czechoslovakia. He mentioned the program that processed them and observed their arrival and temporary confinement there.

Post-1973 declassified documentation includes live-sighting reports and satellite imagery of pilot distress signals. Though most live-sighting cases of American POWs in Laos have been debunked, some cannot be dismissed even though the information was often dated and the follow-up slow, requiring cooperation from Laotian officials. Satellite imagery, from 1973 through the present, of Laos reveals pilot distress signals of the form our servicemen were trained to display to signal their location and situation. Some identification codes do correlate to missing Americans.

Did the Laotians, in their "humanitarian way" spare the lives of those they captured? Are these men still serving some indeterminate sentence doomed to remain in Laos for following orders as a result of a "secret war?"

Laos today is a sovereign nation, and the leaders in charge of the country are those who took power in 1973. The U.S. negotiating position must be changed to reflect the fact that there is substantive proof that American captives were alive in 1973. Joint U.S.-Laotian-Vietnamese negotiations could prove rewarding if decision-makers could be involved. A late but true settlement could yield much information and even some survivors.

Roger Hall is a pre-Vietnam veteran and an information researcher. He has been involved in POW/MIA research since 1993 and was a graduate student at the University of Maryland,

University College, when this article, which first appeared in the Conservative Review, was published.

* * *

I joined forces with Roger Hall in his long work to bring home more POW/MIAs in 2008. Over the years, we have worked together on many POW issues, and most recently he included David's case in his 2008 lawsuit against the CIA for all the POW documents they have not released. There have been several executive orders over the years to declassify the POW documents, which the CIA has ignored. Government stalling is still alive and well; the case is still in court at the time of this book's publication.

CHAPTER 35

My Search For David Will Never End

In 1997, when I would go to Washington, I would always visit my Senator's office. After Robert Dole left office, Pat Roberts took his seat, so I had to start all over informing a new staff member on David's case.

Senator Roberts was on the Intelligence Committee, so I had hopes he could help David. I wanted David to be an important case, hoping it would somehow leak back to the Laotians and they would take good care of him. I worked with the Senator's office until 2006 when I was told by the new chief of staff that the Senator was going to focus on health care and would no longer be able to help me.

In 2003, while in Washington, I met with a young man who worked in Stoney Beach. They were the guys on the ground actually doing the digging and searching for the missing. As we chatted, he informed me that Shelton's and David's case could be solved by the Laotians and would not need digging. I asked him if he had been given David's file and, to my astonishment, he said he had been told to go to the Library of Congress and do his investigation! I was shocked and told him I would send him information I had on David so he would know where to look if he was allowed to. After a couple of years, he was moved, so I lost contact with him. It is a pattern of the agencies tasked with the investigations of POWs to be moved as soon as they become aware that things are not right. After that, I quit going to the government briefings, because they frustrated me so badly. They only talked about remains and not the men who were left alive in captivity. I decided that with the Internet and all the latest technology, I could do what I needed to do from home.

In 2005, I decided to contact the Laotian Embassy in Washington. In our first meeting, I presented David's case directly to them in the hope that they would understand that David was still of value, giving them incentive to take good care of him. I presented my documentation on David and asked it to be passed to their president.

In my second meeting with their Embassy in 2006, they tried to push me off onto the National League of Families, but I told them the NLF did not speak to me or for David, still trying to let them know that David had value.

As mentioned in the previous chapter, I have continued to work with Roger Hall on his lawsuit against the CIA, filed in 2008. The CIA has stalled endlessly in giving documents. That is exactly what Mr. Horbaly said would happen to me if I had brought suit. He stated, "The government will stall and keep you in court for 15 years, running you out of money."

The families of POW/MIAs had tried for years to get the DPMO defunded, with no success. I sent documents to the Committee and eventually, the DPMO was dissolved. The families of POWs had reason for new hope of a real investigation of their POW/MIA loved ones.

We were promised the new agency would work closely with the families of POW/MIAs. The first person to hold the office was a former Navy Seal, so we had high hopes, though they were dashed again when he was replaced. The new agency was called Defense POW/MIA Accounting Agency, (DPAA).

I immediately contacted the DPAA and sent a file on David showing problems with the issue over the years. But they still keep excavating grave sites when it was a known fact that David was in captivity. and his captors knew exactly where he was!

In 2009 I started working towards getting in to see President Obama. All through the Obama Administration I made numerous requests to meet with the President on the POW/MIA issue. When I would write to Obama, they would just send my letters to DPAA. The frustration was never-ending.

In 2012 Senator Claire McCaskill held hearings in Washington on waste in the Pentagon, in particular asking for an accounting for the money that had been spent for years on the POW/MIA issue, with only pitifully few returned remains to show for it. All of the Presidential administrations have told the American public the Vietnamese were cooperating on the POW issue, yet there are even known remains of POW/MIAs that have not been returned. The question of the POW/MIAs has simply been left unanswered by the United States government.

Whenever an opportunity has arisen over the years, I have tried to take advantage of it, but our real opportunity was in the 1990s when the issue gained momentum. The bottom-line strategy of the government is clearly to stall until all of the POWs are dead. I have gone down every avenue over the years from Presidents, Senators, Congressmen, and news media – to no avail. I have been unable to find anyone with any sort of power with the integrity and the fortitude to take up the Vietnam POW/MIA issue.

In February of 2015, I contacted the Laotian Embassy with a "Welfare and Whereabouts: David L. Hrdlicka, an American

Citizen" request. I had run out of things to do, so I thought I'd give their embassy one last try. To date, unsurprisingly, I have heard nothing. It looks like this book is going to be my last shot.

In Loving Memory of Damian Mathew Hrdlicka

In July 2015, David's and my youngest child, Damian, was killed in a wingsuit accident in Switzerland. It was quite involved to get Damian brought home. It took almost a year to settle his affairs.

Wingsuit jumping is a very dangerous sport. They jump off mountains with a suit that has wings. When they descend to an altitude of 1,000 feet, they pull the parachute ripcord to land. Both my sons were pilots. They were also into skydiving, surfing, and snowboarding. David's sons just like extreme sports.

My daughter, Denise, and I were into horse events, mainly barrel racing. Since Damian's death I have lost a lot of my fight, but I will continue to pursue David's case as opportunities arise. I expect by now David has passed on, but I never wanted him to die alone in a foreign country. If he is still alive, he will be 90 years old this December 30. Not knowing is the worst scenario.

Be sure to visit David's webpage powhrdlicka.com for more information and documents. Go to the "Timeline," where there will be highlighted words in blue, click on those words and documents will come up. For more documents go to the "important document" heading.

Damian Mathew Hrdlicka sky surfing

Made in the USA
Las Vegas, NV
05 April 2022